Superships
of the
Great Lakes

··

Thousand-Foot Ships on the Great Lakes

*The long and short of it! This photograph of the **ST. MARYS CHALLANGER** tied up alongside the **MESABI MINER** at Sturgeon Bay, Wisconsin not only reflects the size difference between the two ships but also the evolution in the design of lake freighters over a 70 year period. The 552-foot **ST. MARYS CHALLENGER** was built in 1906 and was considered to be a large ship when she entered service. By the late 1960s this ship had outlived her usefulness in the bulk material trade and was converted into a cement carrier, a service in which her smaller size was a benefit rather than a liability. On the other hand, the 1,004-foot **MESABI MINER** represents the class of thousand-foot ships built over a nine year period beginning in 1972. These thirteen ships were the largest to ever be built for Great Lakes service and their entry into service completely transformed the US flagged shipping fleet on the inland seas.*

Superships
of the
Great Lakes

Thousand-Foot Ships on the Great Lakes

By Raymond A. Bawal, Jr.

INLAND EXPRESSIONS

Clinton Township, Michigan

Published by Inland Expressions

Inland Expressions
42211 Garfield Rd. #297
Clinton Township, MI. 48038

www.inlandexpressions.com

First Edition 2011

DISCLAIMER

The photos, and information contained within have been researched thoroughly but while the author and publisher of this book have made every effort to provide accurate information they are by no means responsible for any errors or omissions to the publication.

ISBN-13 978-0-9818157-4-9
ISBN-10 0-9818157-4-X

Printed in the United States of America

Design by Inland Expressions

TABLE OF CONTENTS

INTRODUCTION

The ships of the thousand-foot class are the largest vessels ever constructed for operation on the Great Lakes. When these thirteen ships began to enter service during the 1970s they symbolized the ultimate creation in the building of progressively larger lake freighters which had originated during the later part of the nineteen century. These ships symbolize such an advancement over previous vessels that even after four decades on the lakes; they have yet to be surpassed.

The opening of the new Poe Lock at Sault Ste. Marie, Michigan in 1969 enabled the construction of thousand-foot ships. Since the late 1800s the locks located in that city have for the most part dictated the size of ships sailing on the Great Lakes. Ironically, the locks located in the Welland Canal which connects Lakes Erie and Ontario, by routing ships around Niagara Falls, are too small to handle the ships of the thousand-foot class, thus restricting ships of that size from trading no further east than Lake Erie.

The inability of the superships to transit the Welland Canal and St. Lawrence Seaway was considered of little consequence to the corporations which constructed thousand-footers, as by the mid-1970s most of these fleets had abandoned operations in the Seaway.

Meanwhile, Canadian shipping firms are heavily committed to the movement of cargo through the St. Lawrence Seaway. This requirement has prevented the construction of any thousand-foot superships for the Canadian fleet. With no realistic possibility of the locks located in either the Welland Canal or the St. Lawrence Seaway being enlarged in the immediate future, there is virtually no prospect that the building of a thousand-footer for the Canadian flagged fleet will be forthcoming.

While the construction of the thousand-foot class contributed to the downsizing of the US flagged fleet following the late 1970s, it also held the promise of the future. When hard economic times struck the domestic Great Lakes shipping industry during the early 1980s, the thousand-footers, along with other ships reconstructed during the 1970s and 1980s, enabled the US flagged shipping industry to remain a viable enterprise.

While creating this book every effort was made to relate the stories of each these 13 ships in a distinguishing manner. This is relatively simple to achieve in the case of ships such as the STEWART J. CORT, PRESQUE ISLE (2), and JAMES R. BARKER all of which were pioneering designs in the evolution of the thousand-foot ship. Rather, it becomes more difficult when considering that the remaining members of this class of ships followed similar design patterns which incorporated common characteristics in terms of dimensions, capacities, unloading boom lengths, etc. Additionally, when the 13 thousand-footers were constructed between 1972 and 1981 several were built to serve the same purpose. With this set of paradigms, combined with the fact that all of these ships are committed to the movement of coal or ore along similar trade routes, there is bound to be some duplication when describing their activities.

This book will describe the reasons for which each of these vessels were built as well as the unique histories of each individual unit of this exceptional class of ships. Also described will be the impact of opening of the Poe Lock upon the existing US flagged fleet at the time along with a glimpse into what the future may hold for the members of the thousand-foot class.

Dawn of the Supership

Since its earliest days, shipping on the inland seas has been driven by advancement through innovation. This is as true today as it was over 120 years ago when the first steel hulled vessels were constructed for operation on the Great Lakes. The use of steel as the basis for vessel construction allowed shipbuilders to create larger carriers than was possible with wood. The growth of lake freighters between the 1900s and the 1960s represents the advancements made in ship building technology along with improvements in the locks and navigational channels that were available at the time of their construction.

In 1900, the largest ships on the Great Lakes measured 497-feet in length while just ten years later there were ships in operation measuring 600-feet long. Ship length slowly increased until 1927 when the 638-foot **CARL D. BRADLEY** (2) entered service. This ship marked the beginning of a time period in which the size of Great Lakes ships leveled off somewhat as her length would not be significantly surpassed until the construction of the 678-foot **WILFRED SYKES** in 1949.

When Inland Steel's **WILFRED SYKES** entered service, she was widely hailed as the prototype of "Today's Great Lakes Vessel". This description could not have been more appropriate as nearly every new US flagged lake freighter built over the following decade incorporated features which had been pioneered by the **SYKES**.

The decade of the 1950s would witness a large number of ships being built for service on the Great Lakes for both the American and Canadian flagged fleets. During this decade, the construction of the St. Lawrence Seaway began to generate the possibility of creating new trade routes for large sized ships. Prior to this, trade between the lakes and ports along the St. Lawrence had been limited to smaller vessels measuring no more than 260-feet in length. With the capability to handle vessels up to 730-feet long and 75-feet wide, the opening of the St. Lawrence Seaway was to change all of this.

Ships built for the American fleet during this time period represent the high point of ship construction philosophy utilizing traditional lake freighter design which incorporated cabins placed at both the bow and the stern. Ships such as the **GEORGE M. HUMPHREY** (2) were considered giants of their day due to their 710-foot lengths. Ships of this class had capacities approaching 25,000 tons which was a significant progression compared to ships built during the 1940s, the largest of which could only carry around 18,500 tons of cargo. However, by the early 1970s, the capacity of the **GEORGE M. HUMPHREY** (2) would be pale in comparison to the **STEWART J. CORT**'s ability to carry up to 58,000 tons of cargo.

During the later years of the 1950s, new ships were being constructed in US and Canadian shipyards which were designed with the maximum dimensions allowed for operation on both the Great Lakes and the Seaway. By 1960, the first true 730-footers were commissioned into the US fleet with the **ARTHUR B. HOMER** and **EDWARD L. RYERSON** entering service for the Bethlehem Steel Corporation and Inland Steel Corporation respectively. During the same season, the **MURRAY BAY** (2) entered service for the Canada Steamship Lines fleet, thus becoming the first Canadian flagged 730-footer on the Great Lakes. These three ships had been preceded by a slightly shorter vessel, the **EDMUND FITZGERALD**, which was built in 1958 and measured just 9-inches shorter at 729-feet 3-inches in length.

After 1960, new ship construction for the US flagged fleet came to a virtual standstill with only five new ships entering service throughout the balance of the decade, all of which were conversions from existing saltwater vessels. Meanwhile, the opening of the Seaway allowed for the retirement of nearly all of the canal sized vessels in the Canadian fleet which were primarily replaced by new 730-foot vessels.

During the years following the opening of the St. Lawrence Seaway several American fleets made efforts to operate along this new trade route. One of the most obvious benefits provided by the Seaway was the ability to move grain from the Great Lakes to a port on the St. Lawrence and then load a cargo of ore for the return trip to be unloaded at a lower lakes port. The most notable fleet on the American side of the lakes to engage in the Seaway trade was the United States Steel Corporation. Beginning in the early 1960s, this fleet would send many of its most efficient units up the St. Lawrence to load ore for the corporation's hungry blast furnaces. However, by the early 1970s, US Steel, along with most other American operators, had generally abandoned this practice and by the end of that decade the presence of a US flagged ship on the St. Lawrence was a rare occurrence.

While the opening of the new locks along the St. Lawrence had produced a significant impact upon the Canadian fleet, another lock building project at Sault Ste. Marie, Michigan would have similar consequences for the American fleet. The locks located at Sault Ste. Marie were one of the most important components of Great Lakes shipping's infrastructure. This installation controlled the flow of all vessel traffic between Lake Superior and the lower lakes. Since most of the ore and grain moved upon the Great Lakes originates on Lake Superior and is carried to the lakes below, the importance of the Soo Locks cannot be understated. In fact, the locks at this location have to a large degree dictated the maximum size of ships built for Great Lakes service since the first canal opened at Sault Ste. Marie

*The **HENRY STEINBRENNER** (4) is shown upbound at Algonac, Michigan during the 1988 season. She represents a standard 600-foot lake freighter which formed the backbone of the US flagged shipping fleet for over fifty years. After becoming too small and inefficient to compete in the movement of ore, most of these ships were scrapped. A lucky few, as is the case here, found a temporary reprieve operating in the grain trade.*

in 1855.

In 1961, work began on removing the original Poe Lock at Sault Ste. Marie which had opened to vessel traffic in 1896 and had since become obsolete. In its place, work began on a new and larger lock which would retain the same name. The construction of the new Poe Lock would be a protracted affair, due in large part to a decision to increase the lock's overall length early in the project. Finally, on October 30, 1968, the steamer **PHILIP R. CLARKE** entered the Poe Lock as part of the testing process to validate the functionality of the new lock. The lock would not be declared operational until June 26th of the following year when the **CLARKE** returned during the opening ceremonies for the new facility to conduct the first commercial passage.

The Poe Lock allowed ships measuring up to 1000-feet in length and 105-feet wide to make the passage to and from Lake Superior. While the Poe Lock was being constructed, ship owners were beginning to explore the possibility of building larger ships to take advantage of the new lock. By the late 1960s, both the United States Steel Corporation and the Bethlehem Steel Corporation had construction projects underway which would open a new chapter in Great Lakes shipping.

Coinciding with the opening of the new Poe Lock was the signing of the Merchant Marine Act of 1970 which provided government backed financing for domestic ship owners to either build new ships or reconstruct existing ones. At the same time, the US flagged fleet on the Great Lakes was becoming increasingly aged, with several ships approaching the end of their productive lives. When combined, all three of these factors led to one of the great periods in ship construction on the Great Lakes.

During the time period beginning in 1972 and ending in 1981, there were twenty-seven new ships built for the US fleet on the inland seas. Thirteen of these ships were of the thousand-foot class, while another seven vessels were initially too large to pass through the Welland Canal, effectively restricting them from trading any further east than Lake Erie. However, five out of these seven ships would later be able to pass through the Seaway following the loosening of size restrictions in the locks of that waterway. Despite this, no US flagged ship has operated on a regular basis in the St. Lawrence Seaway since the early 1980s with the exception of the **EDWARD L. RYERSON**, which did so for three consecutive seasons beginning in 2007.

In 1972, the **STEWART J. CORT** and **ROGER BLOUGH** entered service for the Bethlehem Steel Corporation and the United States Steel Corporation respectively. The **CORT** was the first thousand-foot vessel on the Great Lakes, while the **ROGER BLOUGH** was nearly as large at 858-feet in length and 105-feet wide. When designing the **BLOUGH** during the 1960s, engineers at US Steel had doubts as to whether a 1000-foot vessel would be capable of successfully navigating certain turns in the St. Marys River, which connects Lakes Huron and Superior. Based on this assumption, they decided to build the **ROGER BLOUGH** with the shorter length to prevent any issues in navigating a larger vessel. This ship was originally slated to enter service during the 1971 shipping season, but a fire which severely damaged the vessel during the final stages of its construction pushed back its maiden voyage to the following year. By the time that the **ROGER BLOUGH** entered service in June of 1972, the **STEWART J. CORT** had been in operation for nearly two months and was having no difficulty in navigating the St. Marys River, thus proving that the engineering staff at US Steel had been entirely incorrect in their decision to not build their ship with a 1000-foot length.

While the Poe Lock had made it possible to construct ships such as the **STEWART J. CORT** and **ROGER BLOUGH**, it also presented the opportunity for ship owners to reconstruct their existing vessels by extending their lengths. This proved to be a very attractive investment for many US flagged fleets, with 6 separate companies collectively lengthening 12 of their existing steamers. Of these, the

*The **H. LEE WHITE** (2) was built in 1974 and has a length of 704-feet and a carrying capacity of 35,200 gross tons. This ship is one of 10 ships built between 1972 and 1981 for the American Steamship Company. Her design reflects the modern style of ship construction with square lines and boxy hulls.*

*While many ships built for the US fleet after 1970 emphasized larger designs, there was also a need to construct ships which could transit constricted areas into which large ships cannot operate. One such example is shown here as the **FRED R. WHITE, JR.** unloads stone at Port Huron, Michigan in the late 1990s. This ship measures 636-feet in length and has a 68-foot beam, making her ideal to service both the smaller harbors on the lakes and customers located along confined waterways such as the Cuyahoga River in Cleveland, Ohio.*

*With both forward and after cabins, the **ROGER BLOUGH** was the last US flagged ship built on the Great Lakes with the traditional layout of a Great Lakes ship. This ship was designed during the late 1960s and would have entered service in 1971 had it not been for a disastrous fire which struck this ship shortly before it was due to leave the shipyard. The damage done by the fire was extensive, requiring repairs which pushed back the maiden voyage of this ship to June of 1972.*

United States Steel Corporation heads the list with 4 vessels being lengthened, while the Interlake Steamship, Columbia Transportation, and Cleveland Cliffs fleets each had 2 of their ships lengthened. Lastly, both the Ford Motor Company and the Bethlehem Steel Corporation had 1 vessel in their fleets enlarged.

The rebuilding of these ships involved cutting the ship in half inside of a dry dock and inserting an additional cargo hold section into the vessel's mid-section. Since this new section was entirely comprised of cargo stowage space it greatly improved the carrying capacity of the ship while requiring a minimal investment. An example of this can be found in the case of the lengthening of Columbia Transportation's **ARMCO**. When built, this ship had a length of 647-feet and a capacity of 20,150 gross tons of iron ore. After being lengthened to 767-feet in 1974 this ship was able to carry 26,800 tons of ore, an increase of 33-percent over her original capacity.

With one exception, all of the lengthening rebuilds took place at the Fraser Shipyards in Superior, Wisconsin. The first of these reconstructions took place in 1972 when Interlake Steamship's **CHARLES M. BEEGHLY** arrived at Fraser Shipyards to be lengthened by 96-feet to a new length of 806-feet. The following year her near sister, the **JOHN SHERWIN** (2), received a similar rebuilding. During 1974, three more ships were enlarged at Superior with the reconstructions of the **CASON J. CALLAWAY, PHILIP R. CLARKE**, and **ARMCO**.

In 1975, the **ARTHUR M. ANDERSON, RESERVE** and **ARTHUR B. HOMER** received their lengthening reconstructions. Bethlehem Steel's **ARTHUR B. HOMER** was one of two 730-foot vessels which were lengthened during this period and with the addition of a 96-foot mid-section brought

*The **CHARLES M. BEEGHLY** was lengthened in 1972 to 806-feet, and then converted into a self-unloader in 1981. This ship was originally built in 1959 as the **SHENANGO II** before joining the Interlake Steamship fleet in 1967. The **BEEGHLY** was further modernized in 2008 when she was repowered with two diesel engines at*

*The **CASON J. CALLAWAY** is one of 8 vessels in the "AAA" class. The "AAA" term used to describe this class of ships originated as internal reporting code within the Pittsburgh Steamship Company, which owned three of these vessels. This entire class, except for the **J. L. MAUTHE**, was lengthened to 767-feet during the 1970s.*

her length to 826-feet, making her one of the largest ships on the lakes at the time. Following the conclusion of the 1975 shipping season, US Steel's **JOHN G. MUNSON** (2) and Cleveland Cliff's **EDWARD B. GREENE** arrived at Fraser Shipyards were they were both lengthened to 767-feet over the winter. The **MUNSON** (2) was the sole self-unloading vessel to be lengthened during this period, although 8 of the other ships which were enlarged were later converted into self-unloaders.

In 1976, the single lengthening not done by Fraser Shipyards was undertaken at Lorain, Ohio by the American Ship Building Company when they rebuilt Cleveland Cliff's **WALTER A. STERLING**. As was the case with the **HOMER**, this ship was lengthened to 826-feet with both of these ship's lengths being surpassed only by the **ROGER BLOUGH** and the thousand-footers.

In 1979, the **WILLIAM CLAY FORD** (1) arrived at Fraser Shipyards to be lengthened from 647-feet to 767-feet. The lengthening of this ship, owned by the Ford Motor Company, marked the conclusion of the lengthening reconstructions which took place in the US fleet during the 1970s.

After being lengthened, all twelve of these ships were no longer able to transit the Welland Canal, therefore becoming landlocked superships in their own right. However, by this time US flagged shipping operations on the Great Lakes were concentrated on Lakes Superior, Huron, Michigan and Erie. Therefore, there was no benefit to the owners of these vessels in restricting their size based upon the confines of the locks in the Welland Canal and the St. Lawrence.

With the exception of the **WALTER A. STERLING**, which had been rebuilt from a salt-water tanker in 1961, all of the ships involved in this period of reconstructions had been built during the 1950s. For the most part, these ships have proved adaptable to the changing dynamics which have occurred within the US flagged Great Lakes shipping industry since the beginning of the 1970s. Within a few years of their lengthening, many of these same ships would return to the shipyard to be converted into self-unloaders. In fact, only three of the straight deck bulk carriers lengthened would not be converted into self-unloaders later in their careers. These were the **JOHN SHERWIN** (2), **ARTHUR B. HOMER**, and **WILLIAM CLAY FORD** (1). Of the three, the **ARTHUR B. HOMER** and **WILLIAM CLAY FORD** (1) were both sold for scrapping in 1986, while the **JOHN SHERWIN** (2) has not operated since 1981. The **JOHN SHERWIN** (2) can be considered a special case as a reconstruction project had begun on her in 2008 which was to involve both a repowering and a self-unloader conversion. However, work was suspended on this project due to a significant global recession which occurred later that year.

From 1972 through 1981, thirteen thousand-foot vessels entered service on the Great Lakes. Of this batch of ships the Bethlehem Steel Corporation and the Interlake Steamship Company would commission 3 ships each, while the United States Steel Corporation and the American Steamship Company would have 2 vessels apiece built for their fleets. Additionally, the National Steel Corporation, Columbia Transportation (Oglebay Norton), and the Litton Great Lakes Corporation would each take delivery of a single thousand-foot vessel.

The introduction of the thousand-footers, along with the reconstruction of existing vessels allowed ship owners to retire a large number of their smaller ships throughout the 1970s and 1980s. Many of these ships were in the 600-foot class and had become too small to compete effectively in the US flagged bulk trades in an era of superships. The effects of the lengthening reconstructions, self-unloader conversions, and the building of new ships along with a downsizing in the steel industry beginning during the 1980s can be witnessed by comparing the 1966, 1986, and 2006 shipping seasons. In 1966, there were 154 US flagged ships operating in the ore, coal, stone, and grain trades on the inland seas while just 20 years later, in 1986, this number had fallen to 94 vessels. By the 2006 shipping season, the number of American vessels had declined even further to 51 units. These figures do not take into account the small number of the cement carriers operating on the Great Lakes.

Meanwhile, no Canadian shipping company has built a thousand-foot vessel. This is entirely understandable from the standpoint that unlike the US fleet, the trading patterns for Canadian shipping firms emphasize the necessity of transiting the Welland Canal and Seaway. This is especially true in the movement of grain, which is a major commodity for the Canadian fleet while it remains a very small portion of the yearly tonnage moved by the American fleet.

On the following pages the histories of each of the 1,000-foot vessels built for service on the Great Lakes is presented. They are arranged in the sequence in which they departed on their maiden voyages to give the reader an insight into the evolution of this remarkable class of ships.

*The **KINSMAN ENTERPRISE** (2) is shown downbound at Port Huron, Michigan during the mid-1990s. When launched as the **HARRY COULBY** (2) in 1927 for the Interlake Steamship Company this ship was considered one of the largest ships on the Great Lakes. In 1940, this ship was recognized as the first vessel to carry more than 16,000 tons of ore. A little more than 30 years later this same amount of cargo would represent little more than a quarter of the payload the **STEWART J. CORT** is capable of hauling. After being phased out by the Interlake fleet in 1989, this ship found many years of service in the domestic grain trade primarily between the Twin Ports and Buffalo, New York.*

STEWART J. CORT

The **STEWART J. CORT** was the first thousand-foot ship built for service on the Great Lakes. This ship was built to serve Bethlehem Steel's Great Lakes Steamship Division fleet, with the contract for her construction being signed in 1968. When completed, her cargo carrying capacity was nearly two and one-half times greater than that of the largest ships then in service on the Inland Seas. As the lead ship of an entirely new class of giants, the **STEWART J. CORT** had several unique and innovative features incorporated into her design.

The **STEWART J. CORT** was designed by Marine Consultants and Designers Incorporated of Cleveland, Ohio, and was built by two separate shipyards. In 1968, Litton Systems had opened the Erie Marine yard at Erie, Pennsylvania for the specific purpose to build ships of the thousand-foot class. It would be at this yard that the mid-body of the Great Lake's first thousand-footer was built. Meanwhile, the bow and stern sections were constructed by Litton's Ingalls Shipbuilding Corporation at Pascagoula, Mississippi.

The bow and stern segments were built as one unit, complete with cabins, creating a small vessel measuring 184-feet in length and 75-feet in beam. This unusual looking craft, officially named **HULL 1173**, was launched on November 18, 1969 and was soon given the nickname of "Stubby", thanks to her stout appearance. After launching and final preparations, this small vessel departed Pascagoula, under her own power, bound for the Gulf of Mexico to begin her long voyage up the East Coast and through the St. Lawrence Seaway to the shipyard at Erie.

After completing its long journey, **HULL 1173** arrived at Erie, Pennsylvania in mid-June of 1970. After its arrival, the bow and stern sections were cut apart and joined to an 816-foot mid-section which had been built at Erie Marine in a manner much like an assembly line. Since **HULL 1173**'s beam had been limited to 75-feet due to the width restrictions of the Seaway locks, the bow and stern sections required the addition of side tanks to blend them into the 105-foot width of the mid-body.

Final assembly of this supership was done in Erie Marine's 1,250-foot graving dock, which was the longest in existence on the Great Lakes at the time. As construction continued during 1971, it was announced that the new giant ship would be named **STEWART J. CORT**, in honor of a former vice president of Bethlehem's steel operations whom had died in 1958.

The construction of the **STEWART J. CORT** was to be a lengthy affair, stretching throughout 1971. This was due in large part to difficulties in perfecting her unique self-unloading system. While the **CORT** retains the style common with traditional lake vessels of having cabins placed both forward and aft, she actually has little in common with them. All of the **CORT**'s living spaces for her crew are located in the forward cabins, while those at the stern enclose the ship's machinery spaces and topside unloading equipment. The **STEWART J. CORT** is the only ship on the Great Lakes incorporating such an arrangement.

This ship is capable of carrying a total of 58,000 tons of cargo at her mid-summer draft of 27-feet 11-inches. The **STEWART J. CORT** was specifically designed to carry taconite pellets from Taconite Harbor to Bethlehem's steel plant at Burns Harbor, Indiana, which had opened in 1969. Cargo is loaded

The **STEWART J. CORT** is upbound on the St. Marys River during the late 1990s. When this ship was built, there was some concern as to whether it would be able to successfully navigate some of the turns in this waterway, which connects Lake Superior and Lake Huron. These fears were later proved to be unfounded.

The **STEWART J. CORT** passes Mission Point on her way upbound towards the Soo Locks on a misty summer morning. The after cabins of this ship contain the vessel's unique self-unloading system. Visible in this view are the **STEWART J. CORT**'s original stack markings which were carried between 1972 and 2004.

through eighteen hydraulically operated hatches, each measuring 20-feet in length by 11 1/2 feet wide. The relatively small size of these hatches limits the ports at which the **STEWART J. CORT** is able to load. Additionally, the cargo hold of this ship was designed specifically handle taconite and thus has a relatively low cubic foot stowage factor when compared to other ships of her size which were designed with multiple trade routes and cargoes in mind. The use of a cargo hold with a low cubic capacity is possible due to the specific gravity weight of taconite which requires approximately 16 cubic feet per net ton, while lighter density cargoes such as coal require 42 cubic feet for the same amount of weight.

Taconite is offloaded from this ship by an unloading system incorporating a shuttle boom located at the stern. The shuttle boom system is optimized to unload cargo directly into a shore side hopper, and can reach a distance of up to 40-feet to either side of the vessel. This arrangement allows for the discharge of taconite at 10,000 tons per hour, although her actual unloading rate is constrained by the capacity of the hopper system she unloads into. The **CORT** is one of four self-unloading vessels to be built with shuttle boom installations since the 1970s, the others being the **ROGER BLOUGH**, **EDWIN H. GOTT**, and **EDGAR B. SPEER**. Of these, the **EDWIN H. GOTT** would later receive a conventional boom.

On June 10, 1971 American Steamship's **McKEE SONS** arrived at Erie to unload 17,800 tons of taconite, which was later reloaded into the **STEWART J. CORT** by clamshell bucket cranes on June 18, 1971. This process was done in order to evaluate the **CORT** under loaded conditions during her sea trials, while additionally being used to test out the ship's complicated unloading system.

The sea trials for the **STEWART J. CORT** did not proceed without incident. On July 2, 1971 the **CORT** was forced to anchor in Erie Harbor after suffering malfunctions with her twin bow and stern thruster units. Later, a small fire was discovered in an exhaust stack connected to a service generator. This minor blaze was caused by a build-up of oil residue and soon extinguished itself with no damage being reported. Following a series of sea trials lasting thirty-five hours on Lake Erie, the **STEWART J. CORT** returned to Erie on July 19, 1971 after the discovery of electrical problems with her bow thrusters.

Being the lead ship of a new class of lake vessels the **STEWART J. CORT** underwent extensive testing to validate its design. By August 31, 1971 the **CORT** had completed several hours of testing and it was anticipated that the delivery of the ship to the Bethlehem fleet would take place within a few weeks. However, continuing problems with the **STEWART J. CORT**'s unloading system delayed the ship's maiden trip until the following year.

The **STEWART J. CORT** finally sailed out of Erie on May 1, 1972 on its way up the lakes to load its first cargo of iron ore at Taconite Harbor, Minnesota. When this ship entered service she also inaugurated new stack markings for the Bethlehem Steel Great Lakes Steamship Division fleet. The new scheme consisted of a black stack with a yellow band outlined above and below by a white strip. Placed upon the center of the yellow band was a stylized white hexagon with a dark brown "I" representing a cross-section of a steel I-beam. This revised design had replaced Bethlehem's previous markings consisting of a yellow stack with a black band placed upon its top.

As the **STEWART J. CORT** traveled across Lake Erie, excitement grew in the areas surrounding the Detroit and St. Clair Rivers. This region had deep ties to the maritime industry, with several media outlets reporting on the progress of the first thousand-footer as she made her way towards the lower Detroit River. After being delayed by heavy fog, the **STEWART J. CORT** made her way past Detroit on May 2, 1972 while being escorted by a flotilla of smaller vessels. The following day, the **CORT** made her way up the St. Marys River, where once again she was met by large crowds lining the shores along the waterway. After an uneventful transit through the Poe Lock, the only one at Sault Ste. Marie capable of handling ships of her size, the **STEWART J. CORT** entered the cold waters of Lake Superior for the first time. On May 5th, this ship arrived at Taconite Harbor, Minnesota to load her first cargo. This initial payload consisted of 49,343 tons of iron ore pellets, which immediately set a new cargo record on the Great Lakes.

The tremendous jump in carrying capacity provided by the **STEWART J. CORT** is evident by comparing her with the next largest ship in the Bethlehem fleet during the 1972 season, the **ARTHUR B. HOMER**. The **HOMER** had been built in 1960 by the Great Lakes Engineering Works at River Rouge, Michigan, and with a length of 730-feet and a beam of 75-feet she had been built to the maximum size allowed for Great Lakes service at the time of her construction. Although representing a respectable carrying capacity when it was built a dozen years earlier, the **ARTHUR B. HOMER**'s capability to haul 26,850 tons of ore per trip was less than half of what the **STEWART J. CORT** could handle over the same trade route. The advantages of scale are only compounded by the fact that while the **CORT** can discharge her own cargo by means of its self-unloading equipment, the **HOMER** was constrained by the necessity to be unloaded by shore side equipment.

As mentioned earlier, this ship had been intended to supply Bethlehem's steel making facility at Burns Harbor, Indiana, and it would be the run between that facility and Lake Superior that the **STEWART J. CORT** was assigned to. One notable exception to her usual unloading point at Burns Harbor occurred in August of 1974 when she carried a cargo of pellets into Bethlehem Steel's plant at Lackawanna, New York. This unusual cargo movement was necessary when a fleet mate of the **CORT**, the **STEELTON** (3), rammed Bridge 12 on the Welland Canal during the early morning hours of August 25, 1974. The bridge was toppled into the waterway, effectively shutting down the access between Lake Erie and the remainder of the St. Lawrence Seaway to the east. Since several of the Bethlehem fleet's vessels were trapped east of the wreck they were unable to supply the Lackawanna plant, thus prompting the employment of the **STEWART J. CORT** to make the unusual voyage.

While attempting to enter the Poe Lock on December 13, 1976 the **STEWART J. CORT** became stuck in ice, coming to a stop at an angle which blocked both the Poe and MacArthur Locks. With ice jammed against her stern, the **CORT** was unable to back up to free herself, finally requiring the assistance of the United States Coast Guard tug **NAUGATUCK** to be released after being stranded for over thirteen hours.

*A close up of the stern cabins of the **STEWART J. CORT** reveals the control house for this ship's unique self-unloading equipment. Unlike contemporary installations on other lake ships, the **CORT**'s cargoes are unloaded by a short shuttle boom stored within the structure of the after cabins, rather than the more common deck mounted boom installed on most other Great Lakes self-unloaders. Despite being surpassed in both size and carrying capacity since its construction, the **STEWART J. CORT** will always be remembered as the first thousand-footer on the Great Lakes. A fact signified by the "#1" painted on the front of her after cabins.*

A few years later, on April 28, 1978, the **STEWART J. CORT** once again ran into trouble near the Poe Lock at Sault Ste. Marie. On this occasion she was involved in a collision with the Greek flagged vessel **JOANNA**, while both ships were maneuvering in ice. This incident was of a minor nature as no damages were reported by either the **STEWART J. CORT** or the saltwater vessel.

Following the construction of the **STEWART J. CORT**, the Bethlehem Steel Corporation embarked upon a fleet modernization program which included the construction of two more thousand-foot vessels, and the lengthening of the **ARTHUR B. HOMER**. In 1978, the **CORT** was joined by Bethlehem's second supership when the **LEWIS WILSON FOY** entered service, followed two years later by the **BURNS HARBOR**. During the early 1980s a severe downturn in the demand for domestic steel manufacture pulled the rug out from underneath the American ore carrying fleet. This would directly lead to Bethlehem idling several of their vessels for significant periods during the early part of that decade.

While anchored in the St. Marys River near Nine Mile Point on June 5, 1981 as a result of heavy fog conditions, the **STEWART J. CORT** lost her stern anchor. A drastic drop in the demand for ore carriage occurring during 1983 directly resulted in the **STEWART J. CORT** remaining idle at Erie throughout that shipping season. However, she did return to service in April of 1984 only to run into a serious ice jam which was delaying several ships attempting to transit the St. Clair River. While passing upbound in the lower St. Clair River near Algonac, Michigan the **STEWART J. CORT** came to the assistance of the 600-foot **KINSMAN INDEPENDENT** (3) which was having serious difficulty in making headway against the packed ice.

During high winds on December 2, 1985 the **STEWART J. CORT** and United States Steel's **EDGAR B. SPEER** tore loose from their moorings at Sturgeon Bay, Wisconsin, with no damage being reported. The **STEWART J. CORT** has the capability to quickly empty her ballast tanks, which allows for cargo to loaded at a faster than normal rate. On July 18, 1987 this ship was loaded at the Superior, Wisconsin with 56,251 tons of pellets in 3 hours and 35 minutes, a feat which other vessels of her class are not capable of accomplishing.

As she passed upbound in the St. Marys River on April 5, 1992, the **STEWART J. CORT** suffered some bow damages due to heavy ice conditions. When she later arrived at Superior, a survey indicated only minor damages had been sustained. A more serious incident occurred on December 30, 1993 when she grounded while being loaded at the Burlington Northern Ore Dock at Superior. This was caused by ice becoming lodged underneath the **CORT**'s bow when she arrived at the loading dock, and following being freed it was found that the cargo had been loaded unevenly causing a list to port. To rectify this problem, the **STEWART J. CORT** unloaded 2,600 tons of pellets prior to departing on December 31, 1993. The value of bottom damages incurred during this incident amounted to $500,000 and were repaired the following spring at the Bay Shipbuilding Company at Sturgeon Bay. In April of 1995, the **CORT** would once again ground in a similar manner during icy conditions at the Burlington Northern dock at Superior, but in this instance no damage was suffered.

While downbound from Lake Superior and attempting to enter the Poe Lock on April 24, 1995 the **STEWART J. CORT** struck a pier, suffering some hull plate cracking on her starboard bow near the No. 1 ballast tank. After being allowed to proceed to unload at Burns Harbor, the **CORT** was repaired at Duluth, Minnesota on her next trip upbound.

In December of 2000 the Bethlehem Steel Corporation made the announcement that they had finalized a sale of the **STEWART J. CORT** to an investment group which included the General Electric Capital Corporation for a value reported to be $30 million. The operation of the thousand-footer

The **STEWART J. CORT** approaches the Poe Lock at Sault Ste. Marie, Michigan on September 21, 2008 with load of taconite bound for Burns Harbor. As her dedicated trade route is between Lake Michigan and Lake Superior it is necessary for this ship to transverse the Soo Locks on a regular basis, and thus it is not uncommon to have her make her way through the area 2-3 times a week.

The **STEWART J. CORT** is downbound on the St. Marys River doing what she was designed for, the efficient carriage of ore pellets. When it entered service in 1972, this ship opened a new era in Great Lakes shipping which has yet to be surpassed.

remained unchanged following this transaction as the vessel was immediately leased back to Bethlehem Steel which continued to operate the **CORT** on its normal trade routes.

After experiencing a period of financial hardships, the Bethlehem Steel Corporation filed for Chapter 11 bankruptcy protection on October 15, 2001. In the months leading up to the bankruptcy filing, Bethlehem Steel had begun selling its interests in many properties it owned which were not directly related to its core steel manufacturing business. One of these was the Hibbing Taconite Company which produced the taconite that the **STEWART J. CORT** transported from Superior to Burns Harbor.

An interesting incident occurred during October of the 2002 shipping season. While being loaded at Superior the **STEWART J. CORT** was given the incorrect load of taconite. The cargo put aboard the **CORT** had actually been destined for delivery to a different customer, requiring the thousand-footer to set course for Indiana Harbor to unload. Since there is no unloading hopper facility at Indiana Harbor it was necessary to have the **STEWART J. CORT** unload the cargo into American Steamship's **SAM LAUD** which in turn transferred it to the steel mill's dock.

In January of 2003 the International Steel Group made an offer to purchase Bethlehem Steel's assets for $1.5 billion. This offer was later approved by the Federal Bankruptcy Court in April of the same year clearing the way for the sale to be concluded. Throughout this period, the operations of the **STEWART J. CORT** remained unchanged, although new stack marking were applied prior to the beginning of the 2004 shipping season to reflect the change in ownership.

While stopped in heavy ice conditions on the St. Marys River on the morning of March 25, 2004 the **STEWART J. CORT** was struck by the United States Coast Guard cutter **HOLLYHOCK**. Damages received by the thousand-footer were superficial, while those suffered by the **HOLLYHOCK** were somewhat more severe, necessitating repairs costing at least $26,000. At the time of the collision the **HOLLYHOCK** was a relatively new vessel, having just entered service in October of the previous year.

In October of 2004 it was announced the International Steel Group (ISG) was being purchased as part of a merger orchestrated by European steel magnate Lakshmi Mittal, which involved the consolidation of Ispat Steel, ISG, and the LNM Group to create Mittal Steel. This transaction immediately raised issues concerning the operation of the **STEWART J. CORT** as the Jones Act prohibits the use of any foreign owned vessels to carry cargo between domestic ports. These concerns were rectified in June of 2005 when the operation of the **STEWART J. CORT** was assumed by Interlake Leasing III on terms of a bareboat charter agreement.

Following the management of this ship being assumed by Interlake she has remained in service

*Shown here while downbound on Lake Huron on December 27, 2007 the United States Coast Guard cutter **HOLLYHOCK** makes her way towards her berth just below the Blue Water Bridge at Port Huron, Michigan. She shows no signs of her collision with the **STEWART J. CORT** on March 25, 2004 while operating in ice on the St. Marys River. The accident was blamed entirely upon the commander of the coast guard vessel with minor damages being suffered by both vessels. At the time of the accident, the **HOLLYHOCK** was in her first season of ice breaking operations.*

providing Mittal's plant at Burns Harbor, Indiana with ore from Lake Superior. The only outward change since entering the bareboat charter agreement has been the painting of Interlake's stack colors on the vessel, this consisting of an overall black scheme with a thin orange band encircling the stack just above its halfway point.

The combination of the **STEWART J. CORT**'s diminutive hatches, cargo hold design, and specialized unloading gear restricts this ship on a specific trade route. As mentioned earlier, her primary unloading port is Burns Harbor, while cargo is normally taken on at the Burlington Northern Ore Dock at Superior. The **STEWART J. CORT** is powered by four General Motors Electro-Motive diesel engines capable of collectively producing a total of 14,400 brake horsepower. These engines drive two controllable-pitch propellers which gives this ship a top rated speed of 18.4 miles per hour.

With a general turn down in the global economy during the middle of the 2008 shipping season, several ships were sent into a lay-up status as the requirement for ore carriage plummeted. The **STEWART J. CORT** continued to remain operational that season until December 5, 2008 when it laid up at Milwaukee, Wisconsin. The **CORT** remained idle throughout the 2009 season as the Great Lakes shipping industry suffered one of its hardest years since the 1980s. An increase in the demand for steel production during the early part of 2010 enabled the **STEWART J. CORT** to return to active duty on the pellet run between Superior and Burns Harbor in May of that year.

*The forward cabins of the **STEWART J. CORT** contain all of the living quarters for the ship's crew. This is the only such arrangement used by any ship currently sailing on the Great Lakes. Notable in this view is one of the **CORT**'s lifeboats, and the square lines of her cabins attesting to her late 1960s design style. This ship along with the **ROGER BLOUGH** represent the last ships built for operation on the Great Lakes under the American flag with fore and aft cabins. All other ships built for American fleets have incorporated the all cabins aft design, with the last ship built with a style in common with the traditional lake freighter being the Canadian flagged **ALGOSOO** (2) which entered service in 1974.*

16

PRESQUE ISLE (2)

Of the thirteen ships built for service on the Great Lakes in the thousand-foot class none is as unique as the **PRESQUE ISLE** (2). This vessel consists of a tug-barge combination with both the tug and barge sharing the same name. The **PRESQUE ISLE** (2) was the second thousand-footer built, and would also be the last ship built by Erie Marine Incorporated at Erie, Pennsylvania.

The tug portion of this combination was built by Halter Marine Services Incorporated at New Orleans, Louisiana. This vessel measures 144-feet 4-inches in length, 54-feet in beam, 31-feet 4-inches deep, and was launched on December 12, 1972. After departing New Orleans on October 29, 1973 the tug **PRESQUE ISLE** (2) made her way to the Great Lakes via the St. Lawrence Seaway, arriving at Erie in mid-November of 1973.

Meanwhile, Erie Marine had been busy fabricating the barge portion of the **PRESQUE ISLE** (2), which itself was built in two separate shipyards. The primary structure of the barge was built at Erie, while the forward most portion of the bow section was constructed 415 miles away, at Bay City, Michigan by the Defoe Shipbuilding Company. The bow section was 68-feet in length and was launched on July 27, 1972. This segment was later towed to Erie by the tugs **LAURENCE C. TURNER**, and **MARYLAND**, arriving there on October 6, 1972. After its arrival at Erie the bow was joined to the barge's main hull segment. When completed, the barge measured 974-feet 6-inches long, 104-feet 7-inches in width, and 46-feet 6-inches in depth.

The tug **PRESQUE ISLE** (2) is attached to the barge by sitting within a notch built into the stern of the barge's hull and securely fastened with locking mechanisms, which for all practical purposes creates a single vessel out of the two separate units. In such a configuration, this tug-barge unit has an overall length of 1,000-feet and is referred to under the singular name of **PRESQUE ISLE** (2).

While the barge portion of this combination contains all of the cargo carrying spaces and self-unloading equipment, the tug embodies all of the crew's living quarters, motive power, and navigation equipment. The **PRESQUE ISLE** (2) is fitted with two Mirrlees Blackstone Limited KVMR 16 diesel engines with a combined output of 14,840 brake horsepower, giving this vessel a rated speed of 15.5 miles per hour.

When the **PRESQUE ISLE** (2) was envisioned, the Litton Corporation had been advocating the concept of tug-barge combinations for use in the ore trade between the upper and lower lakes. Litton had purchased the Wilson Marine Transit fleet in 1966, and planned on building a tug-barge combination in the thousand-foot class at its Erie Marine shipyard for operation in the Wilson fleet, an organization which at the time was faced with the problem of having a fleet consisting of several elderly vessels, many of which were overdue for replacement. Thus, when construction began on the **PRESQUE ISLE** (2) it was intended that this ship would become a member of the Wilson fleet. However, by the time this thousand-footer was ready for its maiden trip, the Wilson fleet was no longer in existence. With no Great Lakes fleet to operate the **PRESQUE ISLE** (2), the Litton Great Lakes Corporation was formed which was able to secure a long term charter arrangement with the United States Steel Corporation to haul ore for its steel making operations.

*The **PRESQUE ISLE** (2) is downbound at Port Huron during the early 1990s just after passing through stormy conditions on Lake Huron. This unique tug-barge combination is the largest of its type to ever serve on the Great Lakes.*

*A dockside view of the **PRESQUE ISLE** (2) illustrates the two separate units making up the tug-barge combination. The tug sits inside of a notch at the stern of the barge and is secured by interlocking mechanisms, effectively creating one vessel. When combined, these two units have a total length of 1,000-feet.*

18

One of the main selling points in the tug-barge concept was the minimization of crew costs associated with such an arrangement. When the **PRESQUE ISLE** (2) was built it was conceived that it would be allowed to operate with a smaller crew when compared to other ships of her class. This was due to the differing crewing requirements mandated by the United States Coast Guard which viewed tugboats and conventional ships differently. This idea was proved to be misconceived as the coast guard later ruled that the tug portion of the **PRESQUE ISLE** (2) could not operate safely for extended periods outside of its integration with the barge, thus it did not qualify for a reduced crew size and stipulated that the vessel be operated with a crew similar in number to those of a conventional vessel. In 1974, a year after the completion of the **PRESQUE ISLE** (2), Litton Industries placed the Erie Marine shipyard up for sale as it continued its effort to extract itself from the Great Lakes shipping business.

On Sunday December 16, 1973, the **PRESQUE ISLE** (2) departed Erie, Pennsylvania on its maiden voyage. Upon its arrival at Two Harbors, Minnesota this ship loaded 51,038 tons of taconite pellets bound for delivery to Gary, Indiana. After discharging her cargo, the **PRESQUE ISLE** (2) returned to Erie where she was laid up for the winter. In 1974, her first full year of operation, the **PRESQUE ISLE** (2) set a cargo record when she loaded 54,169 tons of ore at Two Harbors.

During the early part of her career, the operation of the **PRESQUE ISLE** (2) was primarily focused on the hauling of ore from Lake Superior to Gary, with only sporadic trips to Lake Erie. On one such occasion she passed downbound at Detroit on June 9, 1976 bound for a Lake Erie shipyard for rudder repairs. Further rudder damages were suffered in August of 1977 when the **PRESQUE ISLE** (2) struck a submerged object, requiring repairs to the tug at the Port Weller Dry Docks yard at St. Catharines, Ontario, where she arrived on August 21st. After returning to service, further repairs were required at the Port Weller Dry Docks shipyard in October of the same year, which were completed by October 15, 1977. The Port Weller Dry Docks are located on the eastern end of the Welland Canal which means that the tug portion of the **PRESQUE ISLE** (2) cannot utilize that shipyard while mated to the barge. Since the tug itself draws 25-feet of water, Port Weller Dry Docks is one of the few shipyards on the Great Lakes capable of dry docking the tug portion of the **PRESQUE ISLE** (2). While separated from the tug, the barge section is usually docked at Erie which is located just 65 miles from the entrance to the Welland Canal.

During the 1970s, the concept of winter navigation was being experimented with on the Great Lakes. One of the main proponents behind such operations was the United States Steel Corporation which ran

*When the **PRESQUE ISLE** (2) entered service, the Litton Great Lakes Corporation was formed to operate the vessel. This was primarily due to the demise of the Wilson Marine Transit fleet in 1972. Litton was able to negotiate a long term hauling contract with the United States Steel Corporation. This arrangement continued until this ship was purchased outright by the Great Lakes Fleet in 1997. This photograph illustrates the original stack marking placed on the tug when it entered service in 1973.*

several of its vessels throughout the winter season during that decade. Prior to this, the harsh winter conditions prevalent in the Great Lakes region for all practical purposes had shut down shipping from late December to mid-April. One such ship to participate in these late season runs was the **PRESQUE ISLE** (2).

With the onset of poor economic conditions experienced within the steel industry in the early 1980s, the **PRESQUE ISLE** (2) was laid up early during the 1981 shipping season when she arrived at Erie, Pennsylvania on November 7, 1981. With a continuing decline for ore carriage during the 1980s operators of Great Lakes ships began to find alternate trade routes to keep their vessels employed. In one such instance, the **PRESQUE ISLE** (2) arrived at Toledo, Ohio in August of 1986 and loaded a record 44,397 tons of coal. It is also notable that during the mid-1990s the **PRESQUE ISLE** (2) was employed on few occasions to haul coal into the Detroit Edison dock at St. Clair, Michigan.

On April 12, 1990, the **PRESQUE ISLE** (2) smashed into a wall while attempting to enter the Poe Lock at Sault Ste. Marie, Michigan. A follow-up inspection revealed that she had suffered an eighteen inch gash to her port bow, but the thousand-foot vessel was allowed to proceed to Superior, Wisconsin where she received repairs which were completed by April 16, 1990.

In 1995, a unloading hopper was installed at the DM&IR ore dock in Duluth for the delivery of limestone for use in the production of taconite pellets. The **PRESQUE ISLE** (2) inaugurated cargo deliveries to this new installation on July 25, 1995 when she arrived there with a cargo of limestone. Following the transfer of the DM&IR dock to Great Lakes Transportation in 2001 and its eventual sale to Canadian National (CN) in 2004, the deliveries of limestone into this facility by ships of the Great

*A late summer evening during the 2000 season finds the **PRESQUE ISLE** (2) alongside the Shell Oil fuel dock at Corunna, Ontario. At this time she is just about to depart the dock after refueling in anticipation of continuing her journey to Lake Superior for another cargo of taconite destined for delivery to one of US Steel's facilities on the lower lakes.*

Lakes fleet continued without change.

On November 1, 1997, the USS Great Lakes Fleet announced that it had acquired 100 percent of the Litton Great Lakes Corporation's stock. This cleared the way for the **PRESQUE ISLE** (2) to come under complete ownership of the USS Great Lakes Fleet, although she had already spent her entire career in operation supplying US Steel's transportation needs.

While loading taconite at the DM&IR dock at Duluth, Minnesota on June 8, 2001 a seal failed on one of the **PRESQUE ISLE** (2)'s two controllable pitch propellers, allowing an estimated 40 gallons of hydraulic oil to leak into the harbor. Although quickly contained by the crew of the vessel, an outside commercial contractor was hired to clean up the spill while repairs were made to the leaking seal. This would not be this ship's only experience with oil spills as a more serious incident occurred on September 30, 2003. In this case approximately 1,300 gallons of fuel oil were spilled while the crew was performing a fuel transfer onboard the **PRESQUE ISLE** (2) while downbound on Lake Superior at a point roughly between the Apostle Islands and Michigan's Keweenaw Peninsula. While it was originally believed that most of the spill had been contained to the vessel, it was later found that a large amount of oil had been discharged into Lake Superior requiring clean up operations along the Michigan shoreline.

The **PRESQUE ISLE** (2) is capable of carrying 57,500 tons of iron ore at a maximum draft of 28-feet 7-inches. Cargo is loaded through 27 hatches, each measuring 71-feet in length and 20-feet wide and unloaded by a self-unloading system equipped with a 250-foot boom. The cargo hold of this vessel is subdivided into 5 separate sections. For additional maneuverability, the barge portion of the **PRESQUE ISLE** (2) is equipped with a bow thruster.

As of the 2010 shipping season the **PRESQUE ISLE** (2) is in active service on the Great Lakes, serving the needs of US Steel as a member of Great Lakes Fleet Incorporated's fleet and under the management of Key Lakes Incorporated of Duluth, Minnesota. This ship will typically load taconite pellets at Two Harbors, Superior, or Duluth. Typical unloading destinations include Conneaut, Ecorse, Gary, and Nanticoke. Once envisioned to be the first of many tug-barge combinations of her type, the **PRESQUE ISLE** (2) represents an idea in Great Lakes shipping that never received much favor in the long haul bulk trades during the timeframe in which the ships of the thousand-foot class were built. However, it is noteworthy that the newest American flagged vessel currently serving on the Great Lakes is the barge **GREAT LAKES TRADER**. This barge was built in 2000 and is pushed by tug **JOYCE L. VAN ENKEVORT** and while built to a similar concept to which the **PRESQUE ISLE** (2) was designed, this combination is considered an articulated tug-barge (ATB) unit. This due to the fact that in an ATB configuration the tug is allowed to rotate on a fore and aft pitch, while the barge **PRESQUE ISLE** (2) and her tug are rigidly connected with no allowance for such movement.

JAMES R. BARKER

Around the same time that the **STEWART J. CORT** and **PRESQUE ISLE** (2) successfully entered service, many US flagged shipping companies began to explore the possibility of constructing their own thousand-foot ships as well as the lengthening of existing vessels. One such firm was the Interlake Steamship Company. This fleet is one of the oldest on the lakes having been formed in 1913, while its origins can be traced back to the 1880s. This fleet had been created for the primary purpose of hauling raw materials, primarily iron ore from Lake Superior, to various points around the Great Lakes. Since its formation, the owners of this fleet have maintained a commitment to keep up with the latest advancements in shipping on the Inland Seas to remain competitive. Therefore it is not surprising that when the sixteen ships of the Maritime class were built during the Second World War, Interlake took delivery of two of these units. The postwar period would see an upsurge in ship construction as fleets operating ships on the Great Lakes struggled to meet the demands of both an expanding economy and the material requirements of the Korean War. This occurred at the same time that many ship operators were faced with the consequences of possessing an aging fleet. During the 1950s four new steamers were built for the Interlake Steamship fleet. This group of ships included the **ELTON HOYT 2nd** (2), **J. L. MAUTHE, JOHN SHERWIN** (2), and the **HERBERT C. JACKSON**. These ships were joined in 1967 by the **CHARLES M. BEEHGLY**, which had been built in 1959 as the **SHENANGO II**.

At the beginning of the 1970s these five steamers were still among the most modern on the Great Lakes, being surpassed only by the numerous 730-foot vessels built for the Canadian fleet during the 1960s. During this timeframe, plans were developed to modernize the Interlake Steamship fleet to take advantage of the larger ship dimensions allowed by the opening of the new Poe Lock at Sault Ste. Marie, Michigan. This included the lengthening of the **CHARLES M. BEEGHLY** and the **JOHN SHERWIN** (2) at the Fraser Shipyards in Superior, Wisconsin in 1972 and 1973 respectively. The reconstruction of existing steamers was not the only course of action taken by the company as it contracted the American Ship Building Company to build two thousand-foot vessels at its Lorain, Ohio yard.

The order for this pair of thousand-footers was placed on November 19, 1973, with the keel laying for the first unit taking place just less than one year later, on October 14, 1974. It is interesting to note that conceptual drawings released during the early 1970s of the vessels to be built for Interlake bore little resemblance to the actual ships which were subsequently built. These early artist impressions illustrate that the new ships were to retain the traditional fore and aft cabin arrangement, while at the same time incorporating modern design features such as an aft mounted self-unloading boom as well as a rounded bow. However, the final design to emerge would incorporate an all cabins aft arrangement with the self-unloading boom mounted on the face of the cabins. This design would set the pattern to which all of the other thousand-foot vessels built by the American Ship Building Company would follow, with the exception of United States Steel's **EDGAR B. SPEER**.

While being constructed, sections of the thousand-footer's cabins were fabricated at American Ship

Building's Chicago, Illinois yard. These were later transported to the Lorain yard strapped to the deck of the steamer **GEORGE D. GOBLE**. Following their arrival, they were installed upon the hull as it took shape inside the massive dry dock located along the shores of the Black River.

On May 29, 1976, this ship was launched when water was allowed into the dry dock's chamber, which in turn lifted the thousand-foot vessel up from her building blocks. Final fitting out activities continued following her launching, culminating with sea trials which took place in late July. On August 7, 1976 this ship was christened at Cleveland, Ohio as the **JAMES R. BARKER**. At 1,004 feet in length she was the largest ship constructed entirely upon the Great Lakes up to that time, the previous holder of this record being the **ROGER BLOUGH** which had been completed at Lorain in 1972.

The **JAMES R. BARKER** deviated significantly in design philosophy from the two thousand-foot ships previously built. While the **STEWART J. CORT** was built for a specific type of cargo and trade route, and the **PRESQUE ISLE** (2) was constructed to the tug-barge concept, the **JAMES R. BARKER** was designed to be able to efficiently haul a variety of cargoes over various trade patterns. A comparison of the cargo hold designs of the **STEWART J. CORT** and the **JAMES R. BARKER** clearly illustrates the differing specifications that these two superships were designed to meet. The **STEWART J. CORT**'s cargo holds had been built to specifically haul taconite and therefore had a low total cubic foot capacity. The cargo compartments of the **CORT** have a total of 1,647,705 cubic feet of storage space. The sides of the holds are sloped to allow the discharge of taconite pellets onto a single conveyor belt running under the cargo hold gates. This is an efficient method of transporting taconite, but since it was envisioned to operate the **JAMES R. BARKER** in both the ore and coal trades her cargo hold was designed with a total of 2,405,220 cubic feet of space, an increase of nearly 46 percent over that of the similarly sized **STEWART J. CORT**. This was accomplished by using a different ballast tank arrangement and the incorporation of three separate conveyor belts running under the holds

*The **JAMES R. BARKER** is downbound in early spring ice at Marysville, Michigan during the mid-1990s. Four out of the five thousand-foot vessels built by the American Ship Building Company followed the general design of this groundbreaking ship.*

23

*The **JAMES R. BARKER** is downbound on the St. Clair River. When built in 1976, a ship with an all aft cabin design was relatively rare within the US flagged Great Lakes fleet. This ship was built to haul a variety of cargos rather than just taconite as is the case with the **STEWART J. CORT**.*

for the unloading of cargo.

When the **JAMES R. BARKER** departed Cleveland for her maiden voyage on August 8, 1976 she became the largest ship on the Great Lakes, her length not being surpassed until a fleet mate, the **WILLIAM J. DE LANCEY**, entered service five years later. Her maiden trip took her up the lakes to Taconite Harbor, Minnesota where she loaded a cargo of taconite destined for delivery to a lower lakes port.

Early in its career, the **JAMES R. BARKER** was heavily engaged in the transport of taconite for Interlake's customers on the lower lakes. The onset of a steel strike during the summer of 1977, and a corresponding drop in the demand for ore carriage, prompted the Interlake Steamship Company to lay up the **JAMES R. BARKER** at Ashland, Wisconsin. She remained at that location until mid-January of the following year, only to face heavy ice conditions as she struggled to depart the northern port to resume trading. Three years later, on January 24, 1980, the **JAMES R. BARKER** suffered a small fire while in winter lay-up at Ashtabula, Ohio. This incident, which resulted from sparks generated by welding operations, resulted in only minor damage.

During the late 1970s the Republic Steel Corporation constructed a taconite pellet transshipment terminal at Lorain to supply their steel mills in nearby Cleveland. Since Republic's docks in that city were located up the twisting Cuyahoga River, the new thousand-footers were unable to directly supply their raw material needs. To address this issue, a solution had been found in transporting ore from the upper lakes onboard a thousand-foot vessel to Lorain where it would unload its cargo. This taconite would then be reloaded into a number of smaller ships which were capable of navigating up the

*A close up of the **JAMES R. BARKER**'s stern cabin arrangement illustrates the relative compactness of the overall structure. The self-unloading boom is attached to a pivot point located 94-feet from the stern, and is able to rotate up to 100-degrees to either side of the ship to unload cargo directly onto a dock or into a hopper. Also visible are the stack markings of the Interlake Steamship fleet which consists of a black stack encircled by an orange band. This is one of the oldest and most recognizable schemes in use on the Great Lakes, having remained unchanged for many decades.*

Cuyahoga River to deposit the taconite where it was required for the production of steel. This process eliminated the established method of hauling ore from the upper lakes all the way into Cleveland aboard a vessel which was able to navigate the confines of the Cuyahoga. The movement of taconite into the Lorain transshipment facility quickly became a common destination for the thousand-foot vessels in the Interlake fleet. An early trip for an Interlake ship into this location occurred on May 6, 1980 when the **JAMES R. BARKER** arrived with a cargo of 55,000 tons of taconite.

The arrival of the 1980s had ushered in a decade of hardships for the Great Lakes shipping industry. The influx of cheap foreign steel accompanied by a general economic recession created a significant drop in the demand for ore carriage on the Great Lakes at the beginning of that decade. Reacting to such conditions, ship operators struggled to keep their vessels active in a pool of ever decreasing cargoes. During this timeframe it became common for ships to remain tied up for significant periods, while awaiting the improvement of economic conditions. In August of 1982 the **JAMES R. BARKER** arrived at Picklands Mather's dock at Detour, Michigan where she was laid up due to the lack of cargoes, remaining there until returning to service in October of the following year. After resuming operation, the **JAMES R. BARKER** was required to proceed to the Fraser Shipyards in Superior where she received rudder repairs.

While upbound in lower Lake Huron on October 27, 1986, a fire caused by a broken fuel line erupted in the **JAMES R. BARKER**'s engine room around 8:30PM. At the time, this ship and had just passed the junction of Lake Huron and the St. Clair River. The blaze was extinguished by fire fighting efforts of the **BARKER**'s crew, with no injuries being reported. During the incident, the **JAMES R. BARKER** lost power and went to anchor outside of the shipping channel in the lake, two miles north of Port Huron, Michigan. To the south, the **WILLIAM J. DE LANCEY** was unloading coal at Detroit Edison's St. Clair Power Plant and following her departure she arrived alongside the powerless **JAMES R. BARKER** to tow her, in a side-by-side fashion, to Sturgeon Bay, Wisconsin for repairs at Bay Shipbuilding. After a lengthy tow, the pair arrived at Sturgeon Bay on November 2, 1986 where repairs were made to the **JAMES R. BARKER**.

In 1987, significant changes occurred to ownership of the Interlake Steamship fleet when it was spun off by its parent company, Moore McCormick Lines, and as a result became a privately held company with the namesake of its first-thousand footer, James R. Barker, becoming its Chairman of the Board. Following the change in ownership, the Picklands Mather & Co. emblems, which had been affixed to the bows of the fleet's ships since the 1970s, were removed.

A little more than two years following her engine room fire on Lake Huron, a less serious accident occurred when the **JAMES R. BARKER** struck the loading dock at Two Harbors, Minnesota on December 24, 1988, while arriving to load taconite. Strong winds were blamed for the incident which resulted in a six-foot crack in the ship's hull. After a survey of the damage was completed, the load consigned to the **JAMES R. BARKER** was cancelled and the thousand-footer sailed for the Port Terminal at Duluth, Minnesota where repairs were completed over the winter lay-up period.

A few anxious moments were experienced by the crew of the **JAMES R. BARKER** on June 21, 1993 while the thousand-footer was following the **JOSEPH H. THOMPSON** into Duluth. While the barge was passing under the Duluth Aerial Bridge its tug, the **JOSEPH H. THOMPSON JR.**, lost power causing the **BARKER** to come to a abrupt stop in an effort to avoid running into the powerless vessel. No actual contact was made between the vessels, and both vessels soon continued on to their respective destinations.

Ships downbound on the St. Marys River must transit the Rock Cut. This man made channel is located south of Soo Locks and makes for a very constricted waterway for large vessels such as the **JAMES R. BARKER** as they attempt to pass through it. In order to line up for the Rock Cut the approaching ship must make a hard turn to port near its entrance. It was during such a maneuver that the **JAMES R. BARKER** hit the bottom of the St. Marys River on April 5, 2000, resulting in flooding of her number #1 ballast tank located on the starboard side. The inrushing water caused the **BARKER** to develop a minor list before the ship went to anchor lower in the river near Lime Island. After an on-site survey of damages, the thousand-footer was allowed to proceed to St, Clair, Michigan where she unloaded her coal cargo at the Detroit Edison Power Plant before arriving at Sturgeon Bay, Wisconsin

*On May 31, 2010 the **JAMES R. BARKER** is downbound on Lake Huron with a cargo of coal destined for delivery to Detroit Edison's St. Clair Power Plant. She is near the exact spot at which she suffered a major engine room fire on October 27, 1986.*

on April 10th where repairs were performed.

The **JAMES R. BARKER** received further damage to her number #1 ballast tank on April 2, 2003 while downbound on Whitefish Bay. When water was discovered entering the ballast tank it was initially believed to have been caused by a mechanical problem, but while passing through the Poe Lock it was discovered that ice had ripped into the supership's bow. After exiting the lock, the **BARKER** tied up alongside the approach wall to the MacArthur Lock, where repairs were made prior to her departure on April 6, 2003.

The 1,004-foot long **JAMES R. BARKER** is 105-feet wide, and with a depth of 50-feet is capable of carrying 63,300 tons of cargo at a maximum draft of 29-feet 1-inch. Primary payloads for this vessel include taconite and coal, although stone has also been carried on rare occasions. This ship has been active during the 2010 season in the coal trade supplying Detroit Edison's St. Clair Power Plant just north of Marine City, Michigan. When the **JAMES R. BARKER** is carrying coal, her maximum carrying capacity is reduced to 57,200 tons.

Every thousand-foot vessel built for service on the Great Lakes was designed as a self-unloader, and as such the **JAMES R. BARKER** is fitted with a 250 foot long unloading boom which can rotate 100-degrees to either side of the ship. Unlike the **STEWART J. CORT**, this ship was built with 36 conventional hatches, each measuring 65-feet long by 11-feet wide, and thus is able to load at a variety of locations, unlike the **CORT** which is limited from doing so by her small hatches.

The **JAMES R. BARKER** was followed by two thousand-footers built by the American Ship Building Company for the Interlake Steamship Company which shared similar appearances. These were the **MESABI MINER** and the **WILLIAM J. DE LANCEY** which entered service in 1977 and 1981 respectively. This trio was joined in 1992 by another thousand-footer built at Lorain, the **GEORGE A. STINSON**. The **STINSON** was managed by the Interlake fleet from 1992 until 1996, bringing a total of four thousand-foot vessels into one fleet for the first time since this class of ships entered the scene. After operating only three thousand-footers after 1996, history repeated itself in 2005 when the Interlake Steamship Company once again began managing four superships following the operation of the **STEWART J. CORT** being assumed by a subsidiary of the Interlake Steamship Company.

The **JAMES R. BARKER** is powered by a pair of Pielstick diesel engines rated with a combined total of 16,000 brake horsepower which propel this ship to speeds of up to 15 miles per hour. Although the **BARKER** was not the first thousand-foot vessel to enter service on the Great Lakes, she should be considered a benchmark in the development of the Great Lakes freighter as she was designed to operate in a wide variety of trade routes. This was in direct opposition to the philosophy behind the design of the **STEWART J. CORT**, while at the same time the **BARKER** was not as radical of a departure from the traditional lake vessel as was the case with the integrated tug-barge concept exemplified by the **PRESQUE ISLE** (2).

MESABI MINER

Following the **JAMES R. BARKER**, the next ship built by the American Ship Building Company's Lorain yard was the **MESABI MINER**. This vessel was the second of the two thousand-footers ordered by the Interlake Steamship Company on November 19, 1973. Therefore, she was a virtual duplicate of Interlake's first thousand-footer, especially in terms of dimensions, carrying capacity, and propulsion. In common with the **BARKER**, the **MESABI MINER** was designed to operate effectively in the coal and ore trade.

The **MESABI MINER** was launched on February 14, 1977. Following its fitting out, this ship departed Lorain, Ohio on June 7, 1977 bound for Duluth, Minnesota where it was formally christened as the **MESABI MINER** on June 11th. Three days later, on June 14, 1977, the **MESABI MINER** became the first thousand-foot vessel to load taconite at Burlington Northern's Dock #5 at Superior, Wisconsin. This ore dock had been constructed during the 1970s and utilized a conveyor system to load ships unlike its predecessors which had been built with gravity chutes. As such, the new facility was capable of efficiently loading the largest ships on the Great Lakes.

With a 1,004-foot length, a 105-foot beam, and a 50-foot depth this ship has dimensions identical to that of the **JAMES R. BARKER**. After being commissioned into service the **MESABI MINER** soon settled into the movement of taconite from the upper lakes to the unloading ports located on the lower lakes.

On January 28, 1978, near the end of her first operational season, the **MESABI MINER** ran into trouble on the St. Marys River, just downriver from the Soo Locks. On this date, while passing Mission Point, this ship damaged the ice boom in place near the Sugar Island ferry dock. No damage was reported as having been suffered by the thousand-footer as a result of this incident, although the ice boom required repairs which were undertaken by the Corps of Engineers.

When ships of the thousand-foot class began operating on the Great Lakes it was perceived that they would be employed almost exclusively in transporting cargoes to and from the major ports around the lakes. In such roles, their owners could take full advantage of their carrying capacity to supply their major hauling contracts with maximum efficiency. In practice however, several of these ships have been employed to make deliveries into some of the smaller ports on the Great Lakes. An early example of this occurred on October 24, 1979 when the **MESABI MINER** arrived at Conneaut, Ohio and loaded 38,850 tons of coal bound for Port Washington, Wisconsin. In doing so, this ship became the first thousand-foot vessel to both load at Conneaut and unload at Port Washington. On this trip, depth restrictions at the Wisconsin port had prohibited the **MESABI MINER** from being loaded to her maximum capacity. When loading for another trip into Port Washington during April of 1980 the **MESABI MINER** set a coal loading record for a Lake Erie port when she loaded 46,915 tons of coal at Conneaut.

As with numerous other American flagged ships, the operation of the **MESABI MINER** is closely linked to the steel industry. Therefore, when a drop in the demand for ore carriage occurs as a result of a downturn in the demand for steel production it is common for the **MESABI MINER** to spend periods of time at the wall due to the lack of available cargoes. Such conditions were very prevalent during the early 1980s, with this ship spending some extended periods of time in lay-up. In one example, the **MESABI MINER** arrived at the Picklands Mather dock at Detour, Michigan in July of 1983 for lay-up, joining the already idle **JAMES R. BARKER**.

Following the Interlake Steamship Company being awarded a major ore hauling contract by the Republic Steel Corporation in the late 1970s, the **MESABI MINER** became heavily utilized in the transporting of ore into Lorain and Indiana Harbor to supply that customers needs. Although ore has always held the lions share of this ship's seasonal cargo commitments, coal has also been a factor. On June 15, 1985 the **MESABI MINER** became the first thousand-foot vessel to enter the Saginaw River when she arrived at Consumers Power's electrical generation facility at Essexville, Michigan. Since this initial delivery, the delivery of coal into this location by thousand-foot vessels has become commonplace.

On March 27, 1989, the **MESABI MINER** went aground on the St. Marys River near the southern end of Neebish Island while downbound with 48,736 tons of ore loaded at Taconite Harbor, Minnesota for delivery to Lorain, Ohio. This ship remained grounded until being freed two days later with the assistance of three tugs. Although the **MESABI MINER** suffered no significant hull damage from the grounding she did suffer a hole in her bow which allowed the flooding of her forepeak. Following an inspection by the Coast Guard the **MESABI MINER** continued on her trip to Lorain where she was repaired after unloading her cargo of ore.

The **MESABI MINER**'s troubles on the St. Marys River continued on July 13, 1992 when she went aground abreast of Mission Point. The thousand-footer was later able to free itself from the stranding,

*The **MESABI MINER** is downbound in the Rock Cut during the late 1990s. This manmade channel on the west side of Neebish Island was originally completed in 1909 after being cut through the rocky bottom of the St. Marys River, and is used exclusively by downbound vessels. It was in this area that the **MESABI MINER** went aground on March 27, 1989.*

29

*The **MESABI MINER** is shown departing the Lorain Pellet Terminal during the mid-1990s. This facility, which opened in 1980, was built to receive ore from the upper lakes from ships such as the **MESABI MINER** and reload it into smaller ships which could navigate the Cuyahoga River at nearby Cleveland to deliver the ore to the Republic Steel Corporation. The numerous white specks in this photograph are seagulls searching for food stirred up from the bottom of the Black River by the **MESABI MINER**'s twin propellers.*

but not before the rocky bottom tore a 30-foot rip into her hull. After getting underway, the **MESABI MINER** proceeded to the Carbide Dock, just below the Soo Locks, for an inspection of the damage. Later that year, the **MESABI MINER** made her first trip into Marquette, Michigan when she arrived at the Lake Superior & Ishpeming Railroad (L.S. & I) ore dock on December 12, 1992. Since the loading chutes at this dock were not long enough to reach across the **MESABI MINER**'s 105-foot beam, it was required to partially load one side of the vessel before having the crew of the thousand-footer turn the ship around so that the remainder of the cargo could be loaded from the opposite side of the ship.

On October 2, 2002, the **MESABI MINER** went aground in the Straits of Mackinac. After being freed, a trip to the Bay Shipbuilding yard at Sturgeon Bay, Wisconsin for repairs was required. After receiving temporary repairs, the **MESABI MINER** returned to service before receiving permanent repairs following the end of the shipping season. In March of 2004, the **MESABI MINER** once again encountered trouble in the Straits of Mackinac when her hull was damaged by ice while passing through the waterway on her first trip of the season. As with the previous incident, a stop at Sturgeon Bay for repairs was necessary.

Like the **JAMES R. BARKER**, the cargo holds of the **MESABI MINER** were designed with cubic dimensions which allowed both ore and coal to be carried profitably. As was the case with her sister, this ship's cargo is unloaded by opening gates located on the underside of the cargo hold which allows her payload to fall onto three individual belts running along the bottom of the ship. Cargo is then transferred to a loop belt which brings it topside to be discharged onto shore via a 265-foot unloading boom.

*When viewed from shore, the size of thousand-foot vessels can be misleading and to fully appreciate their true size one must get up close to them. In this instance, the **MESABI MINER** is shown in a photograph taken from the author's boat during the late 1990s while it was refueling at the Imperial Fuel Dock at Sarnia, Ontario. Notable in this picture are the square lines of the **MESABI MINER**'s overall design, while at the same time the curves built into the aft section of the ship's hull, another feature difficult to appreciate from a distance.*

The **MESABI MINER** is often utilized to carry coal from the Midwest Energy Terminal at Superior to the Presque Isle Power Plant at Marquette, Michigan. While such cross lake voyages are common for this ship at the beginning of the season, during the spring breakout period, she is also often utilized on the same trade route throughout the season.

The **MESABI MINER** has a carrying capacity identical to that of the **JAMES R. BARKER** at 63,300 tons. Upon entering service, these two ships provided the Interlake Steamship Company with a dramatic increase in that firm's total trip capacity of their fleet, while at the same time reducing the number of ships required to fulfill Interlake's seasonal cargo movement commitments. To illustrate this, a comparison can be made of the Interlake Steamship Company's status in 1970, before the arrival of thousand-foot vessels, and the 1980 season, following the commissioning of the **JAMES R. BARKER** and **MESABI MINER**.

In 1970, the Interlake Steamship Company operated a fleet consisting of 19 steamers with a combined total single trip capacity of 313,550 tons. Of this fleet of ships, two would be sold to other operators at the very beginning of the 1970 shipping season. Ten years later, in 1980, the same fleet consisted of just 10 ships with a trip capacity nearly identical to that of the 1970 season at 306,200 tons. Therefore, despite reducing the number of ships in their fleet by nearly half, Interlake lost only a negligible amount of total trip capacity. This was due primarily to the arrival of the two thousand-footers and the lengthening of the **CHARLES M. BEEGHLY** and **JOHN SHERWIN** (2). Not apparent in these numbers is the increase in efficiency offered by the use of self-unloading technology.

In 1970, Interlake only possessed one self-unloader, the **FRANK PURNELL** (2), whereas by the 1980 season there were four such vessels in the fleet. Interestingly, the **FRANK PURNELL** (2) was sold to Oglebay Norton's Columbia Transportation Division in early 1970. Self-unloading technology greatly reduced the number of hours required to unload a vessel at its destination versus shore side equipment. This increases the number of trips that each ship can make during a normal season, thus allowing a smaller group of ships to move the same amount of cargo which had previously required a larger number of vessels.

The 2009 shipping season would see some of the worst economic conditions to be faced by the shipping industry in many years. A severe global economic slump caused the idling of large portions of the steel industry's manufacturing facilities prompting a dramatic decrease in the demand for ore carriage, the lifeblood of the shipping industry on the Great Lakes. The effects of this recession is readily apparent when the movement of ore for the 2009 season amounted to just under 32 million tons after averaging 59 million tons a season over the previous nine years. The **MESABI MINER** was directly affected by the reduction of cargoes that season, going into lay-up at Sturgeon Bay near the end of April of that year despite entering service earlier that month. This period of idleness lasted until September when the **MESABI MINER** re-entered service, operating primarily in the movement of coal. As of the 2010 season the **MESABI MINER** remains hard at work in the ore and coal trades.

*The **MESABI MINER** is downbound on the St. Clair River during the 2000 shipping season. This ship along with her sister ship, the **JAMES R. BARKER**, allowed the Interlake Steamship Company to modernize their fleet during the 1970s. The arrival of these two ships, combined with the lengthening of two other existing vessels, provided such an increase in efficiency that the size of the Interlake Steamship fleet shrank from 19 ships in 1970 to just 10 in 1980, while the combined carrying capacity of their fleet as a whole remained nearly identical.*

BELLE RIVER

The American Steamship Company has a long standing relationship with the Detroit Edison Company for the hauling of coal into their various power plants. The importance of this relationship is reflected in the fifth thousand-foot vessel to enter service on the Great Lakes. During the mid-1970s Detroit Edison had begun construction of a new coal fired power plant alongside its St. Clair, Michigan facility. This new plant was to be named the Belle River Power Plant in honor of a nearby river which meanders through several miles of St. Clair County before emptying into the St. Clair River at Marine City, Michigan.

The Belle River Plant was designed specifically to burn low sulfur western coal mined in Montana. To economically transport the volume of coal required by Detroit Edison for their new power plant an efficient method of transportation had to be developed. The answer was found in the transportation of the coal from Montana to the Midwest Energy Terminal at Superior, Wisconsin where it would be reloaded into Great Lakes freighters which would then transport the coal to its final destination.

Until this time, the traditional movement of coal on the Great Lakes originated on the lower lakes to be delivered to various points around the lakes themselves. In many cases, these coal cargoes would be hauled by freighters which had brought down ore from the upper lakes to a lower lakes port and would load a cargo of coal to be delivered on their return trip to load another ore cargo. This method was an effective method of eliminating a costly return trip up the lakes in ballast without a paying cargo. In contrast, the hauling of coal from Superior to the St. Clair and Belle River Plants required a dedicated vessel which was required to spend at least half of its time on the route without cargo. A cost effective method to address this issue was the construction of ships which could take advantage of the Poe Lock at Sault Ste. Marie, Michigan.

It was against this backdrop that the GATX Corporation, through its subsidiary, the Armstrong Steamship Company, contracted the Bay Shipbuilding Company of Sturgeon Bay, Wisconsin to build the **BELLE RIVER**. This ship would be the first thousand-foot vessel built at that yard, becoming the general pattern to which the other five ships of the same class built by Bay Shipbuilding would follow. The construction of the **BELLE RIVER** followed a series of other ships built at Sturgeon Bay for the American Steamship Company after it embarked upon a major fleet renewal program during the early 1970s. Prior to the building of the **BELLE RIVER** this yard had produced the **CHARLES E. WILSON, H. LEE WHITE** (2), **SAM LAUD**, and the **ST. CLAIR** (2) for the American Steamship fleet. Of these ships, the 770-foot **ST. CLAIR** (2) was built for purposes identical to that which prompted the construction of the **BELLE RIVER**, in that it was intended that she be used primarily in the transport of coal between Superior, Wisconsin and St. Clair, Michigan.

The **BELLE RIVER** was built in two separate sections, with the keel laying for the 660-foot forward section taking place on March 11, 1976, and its launching occurring later that year, on September 30th. This segment was joined in a dry dock to a 340-foot aft section which had been launched on August 5, 1976. After both sections had been united into a thousand-foot ship, the entire vessel was float launched on February 26, 1977.

*The **BELLE RIVER** is upbound at Port Huron, Michigan passing under the original span of the Blue Water Bridge during the early part of the 1990 shipping season. This is one of her last trips under this name as in May of that year she was given her present name, **WALTER J. McCARTHY, JR.**.*

*The **WALTER J. McCARTHY, JR.** is shown secured to Detroit Edison's dock at St. Clair, Michigan unloading coal in the late 1990s. The hauling of coal into this location was the main purpose for which this ship was built, and today, after more than 30 years of service, it remains her primary unloading location.*

On July 12, 1977, the **BELLE RIVER** was formally christened during a ceremony performed at Sturgeon Bay. At 1,000-feet in length she was four feet shorter than the **JAMES R. BARKER** and **MESABI MINER**, but with a higher allowable draft she is capable of carrying an additional 15,550 tons of cargo. Before departing the shipyard for its initial cargo, the **BELLE RIVER** was required to be dry docked for bottom repairs. On August 31, 1977 this ship departed Sturgeon Bay bound for Superior to load its first cargo. This payload consisted of 56,073 tons of western coal bound for the Detroit Edison Plant at St. Clair, at which she arrived on September 6, 1977.

Following this first trip, the **BELLE RIVER** was placed on a steady run between the Twin Ports and St. Clair, thus becoming a common sight on both the St. Marys and St. Clair Rivers. Since ships carrying coal from the upper lakes are downbound when they arrive at the Detroit Edison Plant they must perform a 180-degree turn in the river at Recors Point in order to tie up at the unloading dock. To assist this ship in performing such a maneuver in constricted waterways the **BELLE RIVER** was built with both bow and stern thrusters.

Besides serving Detroit Edison's St. Clair and Belle River Power Plants, this ship also delivers coal to that customer's plant at Monroe, Michigan which is located south of Detroit. When operating into this location it is common for the **BELLE RIVER** to unload a partial cargo at the St. Clair dock in order to reduce its draft to meet depth restrictions present at the Monroe docking site.

Early in her career, the **BELLE RIVER** was involved in a mishap at the Soo Locks. This occurred on July 31, 1979 when this ship ran into the guard gate installed on the Poe Lock. Although no damage was reported to the vessel, the lock was taken out of service for 15 hours while repairs were completed, effectively shutting down the movement of any ships too large to pass through the smaller locks in service at Sault Ste. Marie, Michigan.

While the economic downturn experienced during the early 1980s caused significant fluctuations in the demand for ore carriage on the Great Lakes, the movement of coal remained relatively constant. Therefore, the operation of the **BELLE RIVER** was not effected to the same degree that was experienced by ships heavily engaged in serving the steel industry directly, with this particular ship spending no significant periods of idleness throughout that turbulent decade.

On November 8, 1986 the tug **THUNDER CAPE** experienced engine troubles while towing the retired United States Steel steamer **B. F. AFFLECK** across Lake Superior. This occurred while the pair was in twenty-foot high seas off of the Keweenaw Peninsula. With the onset of its mechanical difficulties, the crew of the tug cut the **B. F. AFFLECK** loose. Meanwhile, the **BELLE RIVER** and the **EASTERN SHELL** were transiting the area and changed course to render assistance. The **EASTERN SHELL** was able to get a line aboard the disabled **THUNDER CAPE** and started towing her towards safety. The **THUNDER CAPE** was eventually towed into Thunder Bay, Ontario by the tug **PENINSULA** which had taken over the tow from the **EASTERN SHELL**, while some shelter from the waves and wind was provided by the **BELLE RIVER**. The 604-foot **B. F. AFFLECK** would not cheat the breakers as she was taken into tow by Purvis Marine's tug **AVENGER IV**, arriving at the Soo Locks on November 10, 1986 before arriving at Port Colborne, Ontario later that month for scrapping.

On May 25, 1990, the **BELLE RIVER** was re-christened as the **WALTER J. McCARTHY, JR.** at Detroit Edison's Marysville Power Plant dock, although the new name had been painted on her earlier that month. Later that season, on November 4, 1990, this ship suffered a minor fire in its bow thruster room while exiting the Poe Lock. After clearing the locks, the **WALTER J. McCARTHY, JR.** tied up at the lock approach wall for a few hours, before continuing her downbound journey.

Nearly ten years after coming to the assistance of the **THUNDER CAPE**, this ship once again came

The WALTER J. McCARTHY was the first thousand-footer built by the Bay Shipbuilding Corporation. As such, she pioneered the general layout that all of the other thousand-foot ships subsequently built at that yard would follow. Notable in this close-up of the McCARTHY's cabins is the wider pilothouse compared to that of the JAMES R. BARKER. This ship is a common sight along the St. Clair River and at the Soo Locks as she make her continuous voyages between Superior, Wisconsin and the lower lakes delivering cargoes of coal.

to the aid of a vessel in distress on Lake Superior. On October 30, 1996, the excursion vessel **GRAMPA WOO** broke loose from her moorings during high winds at Grand Portage, Minnesota. Aboard the vessel at the time was its captain and first mate. As the propellers for the 95-foot vessel had been removed for repairs, there was little that these two crewmembers could do in preventing the vessel from drifting into turbulent Lake Superior. After being informed of the situation, the **WALTER J. McCARTHY, JR.** proceeded to the area to render assistance. After arriving, the crew of the thousand-footer was able to get a line placed aboard the **GRAMPA WOO**, but the effort to tow the vessel to safety failed when the towline parted in the heavy seas near the entrance to Thunder Bay. Meanwhile, the tug **GLENADA**, and the Canadian Coast Guard buoy tender **WESTFORT** had arrived from Thunder Bay, Ontario. Efforts to take the **GRAMPA WOO** in tow were abandoned and the crew of the excursion vessel was rescued by the tug **GLENADA**. The **GRAMPA WOO** later piled upon the rocks on Passage Island, eventually becoming a total loss.

In August of 2000 the **WALTER J. McCARTHY, JR.** arrived at the Midwest Energy Terminal at Superior to load a cargo of coal destined for delivery to the Ontario Power Generation Plant at Nanticoke, Ontario. Following this payload, this type of movement became a sizable percentage of this vessel's seasonal operations. Another common destination for the **WALTER J. McCARTHY, JR.** is Consumer Energy's Karn/Weadock Power Plant at Essexville, Michigan. This facility is located at the mouth of the Saginaw River where it empties into Saginaw Bay.

While transiting the St. Marys River on September 16, 2005, the **WALTER J. McCARTHY, JR.** was involved in a minor collision with the **ROGER BLOUGH** near Detour, Michigan. Both of these ships were upbound in heavy fog, with minor damage being reported by both vessels.

A more serious incident occurred at Superior, Wisconsin on January 14, 2008 when the **WALTER J. McCARTHY, JR.** was arriving at the Hallet No. 8 Dock for winter lay-up. While backing into the slip, this ship struck a submerged object which created a 7 by 4-foot hole in its hull. This resulted in the flooding of the **McCARTHY**'s engine room, which caused the stern to settle on the bottom at a depth of 20-feet. The water level inside of the engine room completely submerged the ships four diesel engines, prompting salvage operations to begin immediately after the accident. Following extensive repairs, which cost nearly 5 million dollars, the **WALTER J. McCARTHY, JR.** finally returned to service on May 6, 2008 when she loaded a coal cargo at Midwest Energy bound for delivery to Nanticoke.

The **WALTER J. McCARTHY, JR.** is capable of carrying a total of 78,850 tons of taconite at a

*Shown on May 18, 2008, the **WALTER J. McCARTHY, JR.** is downbound at St. Clair, Michigan. This ship has the distinction of coming to the aid of two separate vessels in trouble on Lake Superior in rough weather, while another accident at Superior, Wisconsin in 2008 would see this ship settling to the bottom. Besides St. Clair, this ship delivers coal to other destinations such as Monroe, Essexville, and Nanticoke.*

draft of 34-feet, although in actual practice this ship is limited to carrying significantly less cargo due to draft restrictions at her unloading docks, or the connecting channels she must pass through to reach her destination. When this ship was built it was intended to primarily haul coal and it is this cargo that this ship has remained dedicated to carrying, although an occasional ore cargo has also been transported. To maximize the **WALTER J. McCARTHY, JR.**'s coal carrying capacity, her cargo holds were designed with even higher cubic foot dimensions compared to those of the **JAMES R. BARKER**. The **McCARTHY**'s cargo compartments contain 2,998,075 cubic feet of space, an increase of 24-percent when compared to the **BARKER**'s cubic foot dimensions.

This ship is fitted with 37 hatches placed on 24-foot centers, with each individual hatch measuring 56-feet long and 11-feet wide. Cargo is off loaded by a 250-foot unloading boom which is mounted in front of the ships cabins.

The **WALTER J. McCARTHY, JR.** is fitted with four General Motors Electro-Motive Division diesel engines providing a total of 14,400 brake horsepower. Equipped with twin screws, this ship can reach speeds of up to 16.1-miles per hour while on the open lake.

As of the 2010 shipping season the **WALTER J. McCARTHY, JR.** remains active in her original role of hauling coal for Detroit Edison's plants at St. Clair, Michigan. This ship was joined by a similar thousand-footer in 1979 when the **INDIANA HARBOR** entered service. Today, the **WALTER J. McCARTHY, JR.** is one of six thousand footers in operation for the American Steamship fleet. This represents the largest number of superships to be operated by any single company since these ships began to be built during the early 1970s.

LEWIS WILSON FOY

In 1969, Bethlehem's new steel making facility at Burns Harbor, Indiana began accepting deliveries of ore. This plant, which will be described in greater detail in a later chapter, had taken seven years to build and created a significant increase in ore carriage commitments within Bethlehem Steel's Great Lakes Steamship Division. This prompted the commissioning of no less than three thousand-foot vessels during the period of 1972 through 1980.

Bethlehem Steel had placed its first thousand-footer, the **STEWART J. CORT**, into service during the 1972 season and soon embarked upon building a second supership. On October 8, 1976 the keel for the forward section of this ship was laid by the Bay Shipbuilding Corporation at Sturgeon Bay, Wisconsin. This ship was built without several of the unique features pioneered by the **STEWART J. CORT**, its design being based upon that which was used when the **BELLE RIVER** had been built by Bay Shipbuilding the previous year. After the 660-foot long forward section of this ship was launched on April 28, 1977 it was joined to a 340-foot aft section to give this ship an overall length of 1,000-feet.

Following its christening on June 8, 1978 as the **LEWIS WILSON FOY,** this ship departed Sturgeon Bay en route to Superior, Wisconsin. Upon arriving at its destination, a cargo consisting of 57,952 tons of taconite was loaded for delivery to Burns Harbor, beginning a length of service in the Bethlehem Steel fleet which would last for thirteen seasons.

During its years with Bethlehem, the **LEWIS WILSON FOY** was routinely engaged in the movement of ore from the upper lakes to Burns Harbor, with an occasional trip to Lake Erie. Over time, nearly all ships on the Great Lakes sustain damage while engaged in their normal operations. In June of 1979, a year after entering service, one such instance occurred when the **LEWIS WILSON FOY** was reported as having to receive bottom repairs at Erie, Pennsylvania after striking an underwater obstruction at an unspecified location.

While approaching the entrance to the Poe Lock at Sault Sainte Marie, Michigan on September 15, 1981, the **LEWIS WILSON FOY** collided head-on with Algoma Central Railway's **E. B. BARBER**. At the time, the **BARBER** was exiting the MacArthur Lock at 2:00 PM that afternoon on her way to Thunder Bay, Ontario with a stone payload, while the **FOY** was downbound for Burns Harbor with taconite. Although the 574-foot **BARBER** was just over half the size of the thousand-footer, it would be the **LEWIS WILSON FOY** which received the most damage from the accident. A survey undertaken following the collision revealed that the **LEWIS WILSON FOY** had three holes ripped into her bow a dozen feet above the waterline, while the **BARBER** had only suffered insignificant scratches to her bow plating. After being delayed for three hours, both vessels were released by the Coast Guard to continue onto their respective destinations.

The **LEWIS WILSON FOY** suffered a more serious accident less than a year later when she backed into a breakwall at Taconite Harbor, Minnesota on July 5, 1982. Injuries to the **FOY** were somewhat more significant than was the case involving the collision with the **E. B. BARBER**, with the thousand-footer receiving shaft, rudder, and hull damages. This incident was severe enough that the tugs **CHIPPEWA** and **SENECA** were employed to tow the **LEWIS WILSON FOY** to Sturgeon Bay, where she arrived on July 12, 1982 to receive the necessary repairs at the Bay Shipbuilding yard.

*The **LEWIS WILSON FOY** is upbound at Algonac, Michigan during the 1990 shipping season after delivering a cargo of taconite on Lake Erie. Although this ship concentrated on runs between Lake Superior and Lake Michigan during her career in the Bethlehem Steel fleet she did make regular trips to Lake Erie. The **LEWIS WILSON FOY** was Bethlehem's first conventional thousand-footer when it entered service in 1978. It was later joined by a similar ship, the **BURNS HARBOR**, in 1980.*

*An icy **OGLEBAY NORTON** is shown while downbound on the St. Clair River on December 18, 2005 with a cargo of coal destined for delivery to the Detroit Edison dock at St. Clair, Michigan. While owned by Oglebay Norton, this ship, along with the **COLUMBIA STAR**, were regular visitors to that location with western coal from Superior, Wisconsin.*

Ships operating on the Great Lakes face several dangers. This can include sudden storms, shallow waters, and collisions. During the summertime, one of the most common obstacles for safe navigation in the connecting channels of the lakes are pleasure boaters. While passing upbound at Port Huron, Michigan on October 29, 1989, the **LEWIS WILSON FOY** was forced to take evasive action to avoid a pair of pleasure boats obstructing the shipping channel just south of the Blue Water Bridge. At the time, the **FOY** was traveling without cargo and came within a few feet of striking the seawall on the Michigan side of the river. Although the **LEWIS WILSON FOY** came close enough to shore that its propellers churned up mud and rocks from the river bottom no damage was reported as having resulted from the incident.

The 1980s were a hard time for the Bethlehem Steel Corporation as it struggled with increased competition along with a reduction in the demand for steel due to an economic recession. This had dramatic effects upon Bethlehem's shipping operations on the Great Lakes, including the shuttering of most of its Lackawanna Plant near Buffalo, New York in 1983. Between 1970 and 1980, Bethlehem had greatly increased the capacity of their fleet with new construction as well as the lengthening of the **ARTHUR B. HOMER**. By the late 1980s, the recession in the steel industry had taken a large enough toll that the size of Bethlehem's fleet had declined from seven units at the beginning of the decade to only four in 1987. These four ships consisted of the thousand-footers **STEWART J. CORT**, **LEWIS WILSON FOY**, **BURNS HARBOR** and the 698-foot **SPARROWS POINT**.

During the 1990 season Bethlehem placed the **LEWIS WILSON FOY** and **SPARROWS POINT** up for sale after determining that the ore delivery requirements for their steel mill at Burns Harbor could be fulfilled by the **STEWART J. CORT** and **BURNS HARBOR**. On August 6, 1990, the Oglebay Norton Corporation announced that it had entered into an arrangement to purchase the **LEWIS WILSON FOY** and the **SPARROWS POINT** for operation in their Columbia Transportation Division. By the end of that year, this purchase had been finalized with the two vessels having operated for Bethlehem through the remainder of the season.

In March of 1991, it was announced that the **LEWIS WILSON FOY** would be renamed **OGLEBAY NORTON** in recognition of its owning company, while the **SPARROWS POINT** became the **BUCKEYE** (3). The **OGLEBAY NORTON** became the second thousand-footer to be operated by Oglebay Norton, joining the **COLUMBIA STAR** which had been commissioned in 1981.

After becoming a member of the Columbia Transportation fleet, the **OGLEBAY NORTON** was put to work in both the ore and coal trades. When carrying taconite this ship is capable of hauling a total of 78,850 tons, while its coal capacity is somewhat less at 71,000 tons. These figures represent the maximum rated capacity for the vessel and do not reflect the actual loading patterns which are required to consider the available depths of the channels along the ship's intended route. An example of this took place when this ship, as the **LEWIS WILSON FOY**, set a record for the largest cargo ever handled on the Great Lakes when it loaded 72,351 tons of iron ore at Escanaba, Michigan on November 26, 1986. This milestone was made possible by a period of high water levels on the Great Lakes during that timeframe and also by the fact the cargo was being carried between two ports on Lake Michigan. Had this ship loaded on Lake Superior, as it normally does, it would have been loaded with a reduced draft when compared to taking on the taconite at Escanaba as it would have had to transit the St. Marys River on its downbound trip. As of the 2010 season this record still stands, nearly a quarter of a century later.

The **OGLEBAY NORTON** fit well into Columbia Transportation's movement of western coal from Superior, Wisconsin to Detroit Edison's facilities at St. Clair and Monroe, Michigan. Another common destination for this ship with coal is the B.C. Cobb electrical plant at Muskegon, Michigan. This plant is

*During the mid-1990s, the **OGLEBAY NORTON** sits quietly in winter lay-up at Toledo, Ohio awaiting the beginning of another busy shipping season. The pristine appearance of the **OGELBAY NORTON** indicates that she has been the recipient of a recent coat of paint, which will soon exhibit evidence of numerous passages made through the Soo Locks during the year.*

the oldest such operational facility in the state of Michigan.

While inside of the Poe Lock at Sault Ste. Marie on May 4, 1999, the **OGLEBAY NORTON** backed into the sill of the lock. After departing the lock, the thousand-footer was required to tie up at the MacArthur Lock's lower approach wall so that a survey of any possible damage could be performed. After divers did not discover any defects, the **OGLEBAY NORTON** was released to continue her downbound trip.

Following several years of financial difficulties, Oglebay Norton began to divest itself of its Great Lakes shipping fleet in late 2005 when the **BUCKEYE** (3) was sold. By June of 2006, Oglebay Norton had finalized the sale of six of their vessels to the American Steamship Company. This included the **OGLEBAY NORTON** along with the **ARMCO, COURTNEY BURTON, COLUMBIA STAR, MIDDLETOWN** and **FRED R. WHITE, JR.** Following the sale, these ships were all renamed using practices in common with the naming of ships in the American Steamship fleet, with the **OGLEBAY NORTON** being renamed **AMERICAN INTEGRITY**.

Although becoming a member of a new fleet, the operational use of this ship remained relatively unchanged. While approaching Muskegon with a load of coal destined for the B. C. Cobb electrical plant on September 10, 1997, the **AMERICAN INTEGRITY** ran aground on a sand bar in Lake Michigan. The grounding of the supership occurred at 5:00 PM that evening with the crew successfully freeing the vessel within a few hours. Unable to pass over the sandbar, the **AMERICAN INTEGRITY** discharged 7,200 tons of coal into the steamer **WILFRED SYKES** to reduce the thousand-footer's draft, enabling it to finally deliver its cargo on September 11, 1997.

The **AMERICAN INTEGRITY** is powered by four General Motor Electro-Motive Division diesel engines with a combined output of 14,400 brake horsepower. These engines are connected to twin propellers which enable this ship to reach speeds of up to 18 miles per hour. Cargo is loaded into this vessel through 37 hatches placed on 24-foot centers. Each of these hatches measure 56-feet long by 11-feet wide and are sealed by hatch covers which are removed and replaced by a deck mounted hatch crane running on rails. The **AMERICAN INTEGRITY**'s cargo hold is divided into seven sections which have a combined 2,982,940 cubic feet of cargo space. This ship is able to discharge her payload at rates of up to 10,000 tons per hour via a deck mounted unloading boom. The rate of unloading is reduced when off loading into a shore mounted hopper and conveyor system with a lower hourly capacity. To improve this ship's ability to maneuver in tight spots, she is fitted with both bow and stern thruster units.

As of the 2010 shipping season, the **AMERICAN INTEGRITY** remains active in the ore and coal trades around the Great Lakes. As has been the case since she was purchased by Oglebay Norton in 1990, trips into the Detroit Edison facility at St. Clair, Michigan remain a common destination.

*The **AMERICAN INTEGRITY** is upbound at St. Clair, Michigan on October 16, 2010. This ship was acquired by the American Steamship Company during the middle of the 2006 shipping season after its previous owner decided to leave the Great Lakes shipping business to concentrate on its core operations in the aggregate trade. After becoming a member of the American Steamship Company, this ship was quickly renamed and continued to work on its regular trade routes carrying coal and ore.*

GEORGE A. STINSON

During the 1950s several Great Lakes shipping firms began building new vessels in response to a strong demand for the movement of raw materials on the Great Lakes during that decade. The first ship built for the National Steel fleet following the end of the Second World War was the **ERNEST T. WEIR** (2) which entered service during 1953 after being built at Lorain, Ohio. With a length of 690-feet this ship was a giant of her day, being joined the following year when a similar, but larger ship, the **GEORGE M. HUMPHREY** (2), also entered operation. The combined carrying capacities of these two steamers totaled 46,400 tons, representing a major increase in the seasonal capacity of the National Steel fleet. During this time, the ships of the National Steel fleet were managed by the M. A. Hanna Company of Cleveland, Ohio.

To further augment its fleet, National Steel had a pair of saltwater tankers converted into Great Lakes bulk carriers during 1961 by the American Ship Building Company at Lorain, Ohio. These ships were the **PAUL H. CARNAHAN** and **LEON FALK, JR.**, both of which were rebuilt with a length of 730-feet, a beam of 75-feet, and a 39-foot depth. These dimensions were the largest allowed for operation on the Great Lakes at the time and provided each of these ships a carrying capacity of 24,250 tons. By the 1970 season the National Steel fleet consisted of five ships with a combined single trip capacity of 108,550 tons, with an additional 49,450 tons of capacity being available from three ships also operating under Hanna management.

During the early 1970s, the focus of American flagged shipping operations for the movement of iron ore on the Great Lakes began to shift heavily towards the use of self-unloading technology along with the building or reconstruction of current vessels to sizes which did not allow them to venture past the eastern end of Lake Erie. At the time, the **GEORGE M. HUMPHREY** (2) had the highest carrying capacity in the fleet at 24,700 tons. This figure was less than half of that possessed by the ships of the thousand-foot class then being built for service on the inland seas. Additionally, none of the ships within the National Steel fleet were self-unloaders so they relied upon shore side unloading equipment to discharge their cargoes. The widespread use of taconite pellets had demonstrated that this cargo could be handled very efficiently by self-unloaders thus prompting a transition which saw the virtual extinction of straight deck bulk carriers operating in the ore trade under the American flag on the Great Lakes by the beginning of the 1990s.

Identifying the need to construct a thousand-foot vessel to serve their raw material transportation needs, the National Steel contracted the American Ship Building Company to build such a ship during the mid-1970s. The building of this ship was divided between American Ship Building's Lorain and Toledo, Ohio yards. The Toledo location built the mid-section of this thousand-footer which was then towed to Lorain, where it arrived on November 15, 1977 to be joined to a bow and stern section built at that yard. On July 15, 1978, this ship was launched as the **GEORGE A. STINSON**.

A labor disagreement at the American Ship Building Company caused the **GEORGE A. STINSON** to be towed from Lorain on August 15, 1978 bound for Detroit, Michigan before the completion of her fitting out. Utilizing six tugs from the Great Lakes Towing fleet, this voyage proved to be uneventful with this ship being officially christened at Detroit on August 21, 1978. This ship would prove to be the only self-unloading vessel to ever have been owned by the National Steel Corporation.

Following the completion of its sea trials on Lake Erie, the **GEORGE A. STINSON** departed Detroit on October 14, 1978 bound for Superior, Wisconsin where it loaded the first of many cargoes of taconite consigned for delivery to Great Lakes Steel's mill located on Zug Island in the Detroit River. This trade route proved to be the primary focus of this ship's operation for most of her career thus far. On January 23, 1979, the **GEORGE A. STINSON** received significant damages when she struck a lock wall while downbound at Sault Ste. Marie, Michigan. The repair cost to rectify these damages was estimated at $200,000, and while the **GEORGE A. STINSON** was allowed to proceed she did get stuck in heavy ice on lower Lake Huron on the following day.

The **GEORGE A. STINSON** has had a very involved history with many incidents occurring throughout her career. One such instance occurred on April 1, 1981 when this ship was blown from her moorings on the Detroit River by high winds. No damage was reported to have been suffered by National Steel's thousand-footer as a result of this event.

A more serious accident occurred on April 19, 1983 when the **GEORGE A. STINSON**'s self-unloading boom collapsed while she was unloading at Detroit. No injuries were suffered by the crew of the thousand-footer during the incident, but the structure of the boom was damaged to the point that it was no longer useable. Following the complete removal of the unloading boom, the **GEORGE A. STINSON** returned to service in the ore trade when it departed Zug Island on May 9, 1983, operating without a deck mounted unloading boom until it was replaced in September of that year. Since the internal components of this ship's unloading system were not damaged during the boom collapse, it was possible to unload the **GEORGE A. STINSON**'s cargo via an improvised unloading chute to a shore mounted hopper until she was fully repaired.

*The **GEORGE A. STINSON** is upbound on the St. Clair River during the 1989 shipping season. She is wearing the stack markings of the Hanna Mining Company which managed the operation of this ship for the National Steel Corporation from 1978 until its management was assumed by the Interlake Steamship Company in 1992.*

*While being operated by the Interlake Steamship Company, the **GEORGE A. STINSON** is shown passing downbound at Port Huron, Michigan during the summer of 1996. Although not visible in this picture, work crews were preparing to build the span of the second Blue Water Bridge across the St. Clair River at the time.*

The 1980s proved to be a very hard time for North American steel manufacturers, a condition which had dramatic effects upon the Great Lakes shipping industry. At the beginning of this decade, the National Steel Corporation maintained a Great Lakes fleet consisting of four ships while the Hanna Mining Company also managed one additional vessel owned by the Hansand Steamship Company. Since the 1970 season the total number of ships operating for National Steel's interests had shrunk from eight to five, while the total single trip capacity of the fleet as whole had remained relatively unchanged. The stability of the fleet's capacity despite a reduction in the number of available vessels by nearly 38 percent was due to the construction of the **GEORGE A. STINSON** during the 1970s.

In April of 1984 some of the most serious ice conditions to be experienced in a generation occurred on the St. Clair River. With its usual trading pattern requiring a transit of this waterway, which connects Lake Huron to the north and Lake St. Clair to south, the **GEORGE A. STINSON** was one of several ships which were to suffer damage resulting from the ice jam. While abreast Marine City, Michigan on April 20, 1984 the **GEORGE A. STINSON** ran aground when the water level of the St. Clair River dropped after its flow had been constricted by compacted ice. Efforts to free the thousand-footer by the tugs **BANTRY BAY**, **BARBARA ANN**, **MALCOM**, and **OLIVE MOORE** proved to be unsuccessful. The **STINSON** remained grounded until April 24, 1984 when she was released from her stranding after unloading a portion of her cargo into the **PAUL H. CARNAHAN**.

As the demand for the movement of ore declined as a consequence of the downturn in steel production during the 1980s, a dark period began for shipping on the Great Lakes. These conditions would have grave consequences for the National Steel fleet, with the **GEORGE A. STINSON** becoming their only operational vessel after the 1985 season. With the economic conditions prevailing at the time, along with the general shift away from gearless vessel operation within the US Great Lakes

*The **GEORGE A. STINSON** is seen while operating in American Steamship colors during the 1998 season. Hardly visible in this photograph is the letter "N" painted in dark red on the hull just aft of the vessel's name signifying that the thousand-footer is owned by the National Steel Corporation.*

fleet, National Steel sold the **LEON FALK, JR.**, **PAUL H. CARNAHAN**, and **GEORGE M. HUMPHREY** for scrap during the 1985 and 1986 seasons.

In 1986, the ownership of the **GEORGE A. STINSON** was transferred to the Skar-Ore Corporation, although she remained under the operational management of the M. A. Hanna Company, as she had been since her construction. In 1989, another ownership change occurred when this ship was transferred to Stinson Incorporated, while still being operated by Hanna Company. This arrangement would last until the operation of the **GEORGE A. STINSON** was assumed by the Interlake Steamship Company in 1992.

The arrival of the **GEORGE A. STINSON** into the Interlake fleet brought the four thousand-foot vessels which had been built by the American Ship Building Company using a similar design into one fleet. The other three ships were the **JAMES R. BARKER**, **MESABI MINER**, and **PAUL R. TREGURTHA**, while a fifth thousand-footer built by American Ship Building, the **EDGAR B. SPEER**, had been built to a different design.

During the 1993 season, the **GEORGE A. STINSON** arrived at three separate Lake Superior ports for the first time during her career. This included trips into Marquette, Two Harbors, and Taconite Harbor to load ore cargoes. The following year the **STINSON** made an even rarer trip when she carried 42, 802 tons of taconite from Superior, Wisconsin to the Algoma Steel Mill at Sault Ste. Marie, Ontario.

At the end of the 1997 season the management of the **GEORGE A. STINSON** was transferred to the American Steamship Company. While transiting Lake Superior on November 15, 1998, the **GEORGE A. STINSON** suffered an engine room fire. The fire was extinguished through the efforts of the vessel's crew with minimal damage and no injuries to her crew being suffered. After proceeding to Sault Ste. Marie on one engine, the **GEORGE A. STINSON** arrived at the Carbide Dock for repairs. Further engine problems in July of 1999 would see this ship tied up for nearly two weeks at Sturgeon Bay, Wisconsin for repairs at the Bay Shipbuilding yard.

On May 20, 2003, the **GEORGE A. STINSON** arrived at Superior, Wisconsin where it went into lay-up after National Steel was purchased by the United States Steel Corporation. The thousand-footer remained at that location until early November of that season when she resumed operation under charter to Great Lakes Transportation fleet. The **GEORGE A. STINSON** operated under this arrangement until the closure of the 2003 shipping season.

The **GEORGE A. STINSON** was purchased by the American Steamship Company in 2004 and was renamed **AMERICAN SPIRIT**. Prior to entering service during the early months of the 2004 shipping season this ship had her new name painted upon her hull. Following this transaction, the **AMERICAN SPIRIT** was put to work hauling a variety of cargoes for American Steamship's customers around the Great Lakes.

The **AMERCIAN SPIRIT** was built with a length of 1,004-feet, a beam of 105-feet, and a depth of 50-feet. This ship can carry up to 59,700 tons of taconite which is loaded through 36 hatches placed upon the vessel's deck on standard 24 foot centers. The **AMERICAN SPIRIT** is fitted with a self-unloading system capable of unloading up to 10,000 tons of ore an hour to shore via a 260-foot boom.

Although the **AMERICAN SPIRIT** had been built to a design similar to her predecessors, the **JAMES R. BARKER** and **MESABI MINER**, her cargo hold has smaller cubic foot dimensions when compared to her previous sisters. The **AMERICAN SPIRIT** was built with 2,137,600 cubic feet of cargo space while the other two ships were constructed with 2,405,220 cubic foot holds, a decrease of 11 percent. This also gives the **AMERICAN SPIRIT** a lower carrying capacity than the two other vessels, particularly when carrying coal cargoes.

This ship is powered by a pair of 8,000 horsepower Pielstick diesel engines. The combined output of these engines gives the **AMERICAN SPIRIT** a maximum speed of 17.3 miles per hour. As of the 2010 season this ship is active in the movement of taconite pellets from Lake Superior to the lower lakes, while the movement of ore out of Escanaba, Michigan is also a common occurrence.

*The **AMERICAN SPIRIT** is shown on the St. Clair River in 2005. She is in her second season under the ownership of the American Steamship Company. After serving almost exclusively in the movement of ore into Zug Island on the Detroit River for over twenty-five years, this ship now serves a variety of customers around the Great Lakes.*

EDWIN H. GOTT

Throughout most of the twentieth century, the United States Steel Corporation maintained the largest fleet of ships on the Great Lakes. These ships were an integral part of this corporation's steel making operations due to the fact that they were tasked with the movement of tremendous amounts of raw materials, particularly iron ore, on the inland seas. In 1970, the United Steel Corporation possessed a fleet consisting of 49 ships operating in their Great Lakes Fleet division. This number includes one crane ship along with eight self-unloaders which operated primarily out of Rogers City, Michigan while the balance of the fleet was made up of straight deck bulk carriers.

During this timeframe, the Great Lakes Fleet pool of ships was becoming increasingly elderly with an average vessel age of 45 years old. In fact, the newest vessels in this fleet at the time were the **ARTHUR M. ANDERSON**, **CASON J. CALLAWAY**, **PHILIP R. CLARKE**, and the **JOHN G. MUNSON** (2) which had entered service during the 1952 shipping season. With the average ship in the fleet being capable of hauling around 14,000 tons of cargo on each trip, a low carrying capacity was another characteristic of many of the ships within United States Steel's fleet at beginning of the 1970s. This situation was addressed during the late 1960s when the building of the new Poe Lock at Sault Ste. Marie, Michigan ushered in a new era of ship construction in US shipyards on the Great Lakes.

In 1967, the United States Steel Corporation signed a $20 million contract with the American Ship Building Company to build its first ship designed to take advantage of the increased dimensions allowed to pass through the Soo Locks. This ship was to be named the **ROGER BLOUGH** and had the unique dimensions of 858-feet in length, 105-feet in width, and 41-feet 6-inches in depth. This ship was built shorter than the 1,000-foot length being pioneered by Bethlehem Steel's **STEWART J. CORT** as the result of a decision made by a design team at United States Steel which felt that a thousand-foot vessel would be unable to navigate certain turns in the St. Marys River. This conclusion would later prove to have been entirely incorrect.

The **ROGER BLOUGH** departed the shipyard at Lorain, Ohio on June 15, 1972 on her maiden voyage which had been delayed by one year following a disastrous fire which had occurred just weeks before this ship was anticipated to enter service during the summer of 1971. Despite being smaller than her rival in Bethlehem Steel's Great Lakes Steamship fleet, the **ROGER BLOUGH**'s carrying capacity of 44,500 tons was double that of her nearest competitor within the Great Lakes Fleet. The successful entry into service of this ship, along with the benefits being afforded by it being a self-unloader reinforced United States Steel's desire to construct additional superships.

While the **ROGER BLOUGH** was being designed, the United States Steel Corporation had been a staunch advocate for the year-round navigation season on the Great Lakes, and several innovations had been built into this ship to assist her in serving throughout the winter months. Historically, the shipping season on the Great Lakes had begun in early to mid-April as the ice on the Great Lakes began to breakup and lasted until mid-December when once again the inland seas became choked with ice. The winter season was especially hard on older vessels which had been built with relatively low horsepower engines. It was this type of ships which made up a large portion of US Steel's fleet, so much effort was spent in designing the new class of carriers with high horsepower engines.

The **EDWIN H. GOTT** is downbound at Algonac, Michigan during the 1989 shipping season on her way to unload a cargo of ore at Conneaut, Ohio. When this ship entered service in 1979 it represented a major advancement in efficiency for the United States Steel Corporation's Great Lakes operations, which supplied their mills with the raw materials required for the production of steel.

The **EDWIN H. GOTT** is upbound, without cargo, on the St. Clair River just below Marysville, Michigan in the early 1990s. Noticeable in this view is the relative narrowness of her hatch crane which is stowed amidships. The cargo hold hatches on this ship are considerably smaller in size than those fitted to most Great Lakes ships.

On November 9, 1977 the keel for United States Steel's first thousand-foot vessel was laid at Sturgeon Bay, Wisconsin by the Bay Shipbuilding Corporation. Unlike the **ROGER BLOUGH**, this ship was to be built with an all cabins aft design similar in profile to the pattern set by the **BELLE RIVER**. As one of the design goals for this ship was to posses the capability to operate efficiently in winter navigation operations, its hull received heavy strengthening to minimize the chance of ice damage. On July 19, 1978 this ship was float launched out of the dry dock, with its christening as the **EDWIN H. GOTT** taking place on October 31, 1978, just less than a year after construction began. After its sea trials were completed, the **EDWIN H. GOTT** sailed to Milwaukee, Wisconsin where it had adjustments made to its engines prior to entering service.

The maiden voyage of the **EDWIN H. GOTT** was to be one of the most eventful first voyages of any ship to sail the Great Lakes. On February 16, 1979, this ship departed Milwaukee bound to load its first cargo of taconite at Two Harbors, Minnesota. This marked the first time that a Great Lakes freighter had began its maiden voyage during the middle of the winter season.

After joining the **PHILIP R. CLARKE**, **CASON J. CALLAWAY**, and **JOHN G. MUNSON** (2) the **EDWIN H. GOTT** attempted its first transit of Lake Superior during some of the heaviest ice conditions experienced throughout the entire winter navigation program of the 1970s. With the exception of the **JOHN G. MUNSON** (2) every ship in the convoy suffered some form of damage while crossing the lake, with the **EDWIN H. GOTT** suffering the most serious damage sustained by any of the ships.

While encountering ice on Lake Superior, with thicknesses of up to 16-inches, the **EDWIN H. GOTT**'s hull had been punctured near the bow. An inspection made to this vessel after it finally arrived at Two Harbors revealed that it had also lost one of its twin rudders while the post of the surviving rudder was also found to have been damaged. Compounding these injuries was internal structural damage caused when some of the thousand-footer's ballast tanks froze, creating buckling in the cargo hold's plating.

In such a state, the **EDWIN H. GOTT** was unable to load at Two Harbors, remaining there until April 21, 1979 when following repairs she finally departed with 59,375 tons of taconite bound for Gary, Indiana. This would not be the end of the **EDWIN H. GOTT**'s troubles on this voyage as she lost an anchor along with 300-feet of chain in the St. Marys River below the Soo Locks while attempting to take on supplies two days later.

*When built, the **EDWIN H. GOTT** was fitted with a shuttle type unloading conveyor similar in concept to those fitted to the **ROGER BLOUGH** and **STEWART J. CORT**. This gave the **GOTT**'s topside an uncluttered appearance resembling that of a straight deck gearless bulk freighter. However, with such an installation this ship was prohibited from unloading at most locations which did not have an compatible receiving hopper arrangement. Later in her career this issue was addressed when she returned to her builder's yard to receive a traditional unloading boom. The **EDWIN H. GOTT** has a near sister ship, the **EDGAR B. SPEER**, which was also built with a shuttle conveyor. As of the 2010 shipping season the **SPEER** retains her original unloading arrangement having not received a boom similar to that given to the **EDWIN H. GOTT**. After the **GOTT** was modified, it became common for her to visit various ports around the lakes at which she had previously been unable to unload.*

After her spate of initial troubles were over, the **EDWIN H. GOTT** soon settled into her intended role of hauling ore from Lake Superior to United States Steel's facilities located at both Gary and Conneaut, Ohio. As this ship was intended to operate exclusively in this trade route it was fitted with an unconventional unloading apparatus. Rather than being equipped with typical a topside unloading boom, the **EDWIN H. GOTT** received a shuttle boom similar in concept to those previously installed on the **ROGER BLOUGH** and the **STEWART J. CORT**. The shuttle boom fitted to this carrier was capable of reaching up to 52-feet to either side of the vessel to unload cargo into a shore side hopper. This limited the number of unloading ports that this ship could discharge her cargo, but as she had been built for a specific purpose this was of little consequence at the time. As will be detailed later, changing operational dynamics later in this ship's career would lead to the modification of its unloading system.

While the **EDWIN H. GOTT** was being constructed at Sturgeon Bay, a similar vessel was being built simultaneously by the American Ship Building Company at Lorain, Ohio. This ship, which will be described in a later section, was to become the **EDGAR B. SPEER**. During the 1970s the United States Steel Corporation underwent a fleet modernization program. Besides the commissioning of two thousand-foot ships along with the slightly smaller **ROGER BLOUGH**, this fleet also modernized all four of their vessels which had been built during the 1950s with lengthening reconstructions. These re-buildings had the effect of limiting these ships from operating any further east than Lake Erie, but the benefits of being able to carry 30 percent more cargo per trip more than made up for the inability to make trips up the St. Lawrence Seaway. Such voyages had been common during the 1960s as US Steel employed several of its ships on runs through the Seaway, but by the mid-1970s shipping patterns such as this had been generally abandoned by the company.

The improvements made in the Great Lakes Fleet, along with the chartering of the thousand-foot **PRESQUE ISLE** (2), during this timeframe allowed the retirement of several vessels which had reached the end of their operational careers. By the 1980 shipping season, the number of ships in this fleet had dropped to 39 compared to 49 it had owned just ten years earlier. At the same time the combined single trip capacity of the Great Lakes Fleet had risen to 803,595 tons, an increase of nearly 14 percent from the 1970 season.

As mentioned on the previous page, the fitting of a conventional unloading boom allowed the EDWIN H. GOTT to operate in new trading patterns. One such location at which this ship had previously been unable to unload was Nanticoke, Ontario. It is that port in which she is seen during the 1996 shipping season. Prior to receiving a conventional boom, this ship had been forced to unload its cargoes consigned to this port into a smaller vessel which then transferred it to the shore side hopper.

*The **EDWIN H. GOTT** is downbound under the twin spans of the Blue Water Bridges at Port Huron, Michigan on December 12, 2009. On her voyage downbound from Lake Superior the **EDWIN H. GOTT** has managed to pick up a light coating of ice on her bow.*

December has been a particularly hard month for the **EDWIN H. GOTT** on the St. Marys River. On Christmas Day of 1980, this ship is recorded as having been stuck in the Poe Lock for fourteen hours before finally being able to continue on her voyage. Three years later, on December 27, 1983, the **EDWIN H. GOTT** once again ran into trouble on the St. Marys River when she went aground near Neebish Island while downbound with taconite bound for Gary. After she offloaded a portion of her cargo into American Steamship's **ROGER M. KYES**, the **GOTT** was refloated and continued onwards to Gary to finish unloading before being repaired at Sturgeon Bay, Wisconsin.

In August of 1986, a labor strike against the United States Steel Corporation caused the **EDWIN H. GOTT** to be idled at Milwaukee. This same strike also sent each of the ships active in the ore trade for the Great Lakes Fleet to wall as the demand for raw materials evaporated. This labor disagreement would last until April of the following year when the longest strike in the steel giant's history finally came to an end, allowing the **EDWIN H. GOTT** to return to service the following month.

The **EDWIN H. GOTT**'s troubles on the St. Marys River continued on November 18, 1987 when this ship struck bottom near the entrance to the Rock Cut. During the incident this ship's hull was pierced below the waterline, allowing some flooding of her forepeak. After temporary repair measures were taken, the United States Coast Guard allowed the supership to proceed to Gary with its cargo before receiving permanent repairs at the Bay Shipbuilding Corporation.

As she was lining up to enter the Poe Lock on April 17, 1988, high winds caused the **EDWIN H. GOTT** to strike the upbound approach wall to the lock, causing a 12-foot gash in the starboard side of her hull. Since the damage was above the waterline, the **EDWIN H. GOTT** was allowed to proceed to Duluth to be repaired. After the damage was rectified by a work crew from the Fraser Shipyards, this thousand-footer departed on April 21st, bound for Two Harbors.

In 1988, the United States Steel Corporation sold its shipping operations to Blackstone Partners, Incorporated. After being sold, the ships of the Great Lakes Fleet were given a new color scheme in 1990. The only noticeable changes made to the **EDWIN H. GOTT** was the addition of a pair of gray and black stripes on both sides of the vessel's hull just aft of the bow. Following this transaction the trade patterns of this ship remained unchanged as she continued to supply US Steel with its raw material transportation needs.

The **EDWIN H. GOTT** arrived in Duluth on April 23, 1990 after one of its twin engines suffered a broken crankshaft at Two Harbors. Four days later the **ROGER BLOUGH** arrived alongside the **GOTT**, which was tied up at Duluth's Port Terminal, and transferred some supplies to the disabled thousand-footer. Before departing, the **ROGER BLOUGH** also received some of the **EDWIN H. GOTT**'s cargo which was offloaded with her shuttle boom directly into the **BLOUGH**'s cargo hold. The **EDWIN H. GOTT** finally departed Duluth on May 3rd, operating on one engine. This vessel went on to sail throughout the summer months of the 1990 season with only one operational engine while awaiting the delivery of a new crankshaft. In such a condition, the United States Coast Guard mandated that this ship was required to be escorted by two tugs while transiting the St. Marys River. It was during one of these trips that this ship came close to making contact with P&H Shipping's **OAKGLEN** (2) just above the Soo Locks on June 10, 1990. This occurrence took place when the upbound **OAKGLEN** (2)

A stern view of the ***EDWIN H. GOTT*** *illustrates her common appearance to the thousand-foot vessels built by the Bay Shipbuilding Corporation. This ship was part of a fleet renewal process which took place in the United States Steel's Great Lakes Fleet during the 1970s which, when combined with other factors, led to the size of this fleet declining from 49 units in 1970 to only 12 by the 1990 shipping season.*

was blown across the channel nearly colliding with the downbound **EDWIN H. GOTT** and her tug escorts.

On November 30, 1990 Canada Steamship Line's **TARANTAU** came to the aid of two fishermen whose boat had become disabled in Whitefish Bay. This rescue was complicated by eight-foot waves which were present in the area during the time due to high winds. In an effort to provide some shelter from the heavy seas, the **EDWIN H. GOTT**, which was upbound at the time, positioned itself to provide a lee from the elements to assist the crew of the **TARANTAU** as they rescued the fishermen.

On April 3, 1992, while departing her dock at Duluth, the **EDWIN H. GOTT** suffered the loss of her starboard rudder after striking a submerged object. When the rudder became detached, the starboard shaft was moving so each of the blades on that propeller were damaged, requiring them to be replaced before the **GOTT** returned to service. On April 6, 1992, the **EDWIN H. GOTT** departed Duluth after a spare rudder was installed along with the replacement of the damaged propeller blades.

At the conclusion of her 1995 shipping season, the **EDWIN H. GOTT** arrived at the Bay Shipbuilding Corporation in Sturgeon Bay where her shuttle type unloading boom was removed and replaced by a more conventional 280-foot boom of tubular construction. This reconstruction allowed the **EDWIN H. GOTT** to unload at virtually any location around the Great Lakes which is accessible to a vessel of her size. Although this ship remained committed primarily to the delivery of taconite to its usual unloading ports of Gary and Conneaut following the installation of the new boom, trips into other locations such as Lorain and Nanticoke, Ontario also became common as this ship demonstrated her new versatility.

During October of 2003 the Blackstone Group entered into a sales agreement with Canadian National

*The square lines of the **EDWIN H. GOTT** represent the design philosophy of obtaining the maximum efficiency in the transporting of iron ore on the Great Lakes. During her construction, little attention was given to incorporate features in common with traditional Great Lakes freighters built prior to the 1970s.*

involving its transportation based properties. Included in this transaction was the Great Lakes Fleet's group of ships. In May of 2004, the management of the Great Lakes Fleet was assumed by Key Lakes Incorporated of Duluth, Minnesota.

In 2003, the United States Steel Corporation purchased the assets of the National Steel Corporation. Following this transaction, the **EDWIN H. GOTT** became a familiar sight unloading ore at Zug Island in River Rouge, Michigan just south of Detroit.

While downbound on the St. Marys River on December 9, 2009, the **EDWIN H. GOTT** went aground south of Neebish Island when the water level in the river dropped due to high winds. In an effort to free the stranded thousand-footer, four tugs were called to the scene. These were the Purvis Marine tugs **ANGLIAN LADY**, and **AVENGER IV** which were later joined by Great Lakes Towing's **FLORIDA**, and **MISSOURI**. Despite the concerted efforts of the tugs, the **EDWIN H. GOTT** did not float free until the water level in the St. Marys River rose during the early morning hours of December 10, 2009.

The **EDWIN H. GOTT** has a maximum carrying capacity of 74,100 tons of taconite, although in normal operation she carries marginally smaller payloads. The ship is loaded through twenty hatches which are significantly smaller than the conventional hatches fitted to many of the other thousand-footers built for service on the Great Lakes. Each of these hatches measure 28 feet by 11 feet and were designed with the intent of this ship loading only at specific locations.

This ship is currently powered by a pair of Enterprise DMRV-16-4 diesel engines which together produce 19,500 brake horsepower. This makes the **EDWIN H. GOTT** the most powerful ship on the Great Lakes while also giving this ship a maximum speed of 16 miles per hour. During the 2010 shipping season it was announced that the **EDWIN H. GOTT** would receive a repowering over the winter lay-up period following the end of the season with new environmentally friendly diesel engines. This overhaul, which is to take place at Sturgeon Bay, was partially supported by the rewarding of a $750,000 grant by the Environmental Protection Agency (EPA) as part of a program to reduce emissions from thousand-foot vessels on the Great Lakes.

As of the 2010 shipping season, the **EDWIN H. GOTT** continues to operate primarily in the trade route for which she was built. During the regular shipping season this ship will be kept busy hauling ore from Lake Superior, with Two Harbors being the most common loading port, to US Steel's manufacturing facilities on the lower lakes. With the before mentioned repowering of this vessel taking place during the 2010-11 winter lay-up it can be expected that the **EDWIN H. GOTT** will continue to operate for several more decades on the Great Lakes.

INDIANA HARBOR

During the 1970s several US flagged shipping firms on the Great Lakes pursued fleet modernization programs through the re-fitting of existing vessels and the investment into the construction of new units. It would be during this timeframe that the American Steamship Company would transform its fleet with the construction of no less than 10 new diesel powered ships. This group of vessels were built to operate in a wide array of trade routes with the smallest measuring 634-feet 10-inches which were intended for use in the numerous tight confines around the lakes while at the same time two new thousand-foot vessels were also constructed for use in long-haul ore and coal trades. The first new vessels built for the American Steamship fleet during this modernization program entered service during the 1973 shipping season when both the **ROGER M. KYES** and **CHARLES E. WILSON** began trading. Following the 1973 season, the American Steamship fleet placed a new vessel into service every year until the last ship built thus far for this fleet, the **AMERICAN REPUBLIC**, was commissioned in 1981. In all, this building program totally modernized the American Steamship fleet with the total single trip capacity of the new ships as a whole equaling 408,500 tons.

As mentioned earlier, two out of the ten ships built for American Steamship during this time period were members of the thousand-foot class. The first of these was the **BELLE RIVER** which was also the first thousand-foot vessel built by the Bay Shipbuilding Corporation at Sturgeon Bay, Wisconsin when it was completed in 1977. The keel for American Steamship's second thousand-footer was laid on August 9, 1978 at the same shipyard. This ship was launched on March 19, 1979 and christened as the **INDIANA HARBOR** on July 11th of that same year.

Following the completion of its sea trials, the **INDIANA HARBOR** departed the shipyard on August 29, 1979 bound for Two Harbors, Minnesota to load a cargo of iron ore for delivery to Indiana Harbor, Indiana. As its name implies, this ship was built primarily for the transport of taconite into that port to serve the material transportation needs of the Inland Steel Company. Despite being built for this type of movement, the **INDIANA HARBOR** is also able to operate effectively outside of the ore trade in the carriage of both stone and coal, roles in which she has been employed on several occasions during her career.

The **INDIANA HARBOR** is similar in most respects to her predecessor in the American Steamship fleet, the **BELLE RIVER**, with identical dimensions and carrying capacities. Also in common with the previous vessel, the **INDIANA HARBOR** has also become heavily utilized in the movement of western coal from Superior, Wisconsin to Detroit Edison's power plants in Southeast Michigan.

Shortly after entering service, the **INDIANA HARBOR** was damaged on October 16, 1979 when she overran her own anchor chain while undergoing ballast tank repairs in the St. Marys River near Sault Ste. Marie, Michigan. This resulted in a two-by-three foot hole being created in her bow. After off-loading some of her cargo of taconite in order to bring the damaged area above the waterline, the **INDIANA HARBOR** resumed her voyage to Indiana Harbor where she was repaired.

As with most other US flagged ships on the Great Lakes, the **INDIANA HARBOR** was idled from time to time during the early half of the 1980s due to a lack of cargoes. One of the worst shipping years, in the terms of ore movement, during that decade was the 1982 season when the amount of ore carried on the Great Lakes plummeted to 38,512,574 gross tons, a decline of nearly half when compared with the previous season. It would be during the middle of this season that the **INDIANA HARBOR** was noted as spending some extended time in lay-up at Ashland, Wisconsin due to lack of work.

Such reductions in the ore trade created the circumstances in which thousand-footers were employed to carry cargoes into ports in which they had not been originally designed to operate. In one example, the **INDIANA HARBOR** was utilized to carry a cargo of stone into Fairport, Ohio on May 20, 1984. This marked the first time that a thousand-foot ship had called upon that harbor which is located twenty miles east of Cleveland, Ohio.

The **INDIANA HARBOR** is no stranger to setting cargo records on the Great Lakes. In September of 1979 this ship set a milestone for the largest shipment on the lakes up to that time after loading 70,171 tons of taconite at Two Harbors, Minnesota. Ore would not be the only cargo in which the **INDIANA HARBOR** would set new benchmarks as coal would be another commodity that this ship excels in carrying. On August 13, 1986 the **INDIANA HARBOR** loaded a record cargo at the port of Toledo when a 55,047 tons of coal was taken aboard for delivery to Marquette, Michigan. A little more than two years later, on September 3, 1988, the **INDIANA HARBOR** set another record for northbound coal on Lake Erie when she was loaded with 59,058 tons of the fossil fuel at Sandusky, Ohio. As was the case with her previous Lake Erie cargo record, this load was also consigned for delivery to Marquette, Michigan.

In August of 1982, the **INDIANA HARBOR** became the first US flagged ship on the Great Lakes to receive satellite communications. This included the addition of an antenna housed inside of a large white dome on the top of the starboard side of her pilothouse, which made the **INDIANA HARBOR** visually distinguishable at a distance from her sister ship, the **BELLE RIVER**.

*On May 11, 2010 the **INDIANA HARBOR** is downbound on the St. Marys River just south of the Soo Locks at Mission Point. This thousand-footer will make several trips through this particular area during the shipping season carrying either iron ore pellets or western coal from the upper lakes to the lower lakes.*

*A sunny morning during the 2001 shipping season finds the **INDIANA HARBOR** making her way up the St. Clair River at Marine City, Michigan. Although this ship was built primarily to haul taconite into Indiana Harbor, Indiana it is often utilized to carry cargoes to a variety of other destinations.*

While exiting the Poe Lock, upbound, at Sault Ste. Marie on November 28, 1983 the **INDIANA HARBOR** collided with the downbound salt water vessel **ANANGEL SPIRIT**. This occurred after the Greek flagged ship careened off of a pier, bringing her into contact with the thousand-footer. The **INDIANA HARBOR** received an 8-foot tear in her hull, while the **ANANGEL SPIRIT** received only an indentation in her hull which measured approximately 8-feet in length.

While departing Duluth, Minnesota on April 14, 1985 the **INDIANA HARBOR** ran aground near the Aerial Lift Bridge. Within four hours, the thousand-footer was released from her stranding with no damage being reported as having resulted from this incident. Later in the same season, on May 11, 1985, the **INDIANA HARBOR** made a test run into the Algoma Steel Mill at Sault Ste. Marie, Ontario to establish that a thousand-foot ship could successfully dock at that facility. During this voyage the **INDIANA HARBOR** did not carry any cargo as the trip was made solely to identify the requirements for the operation of thousand-footers into this location.

After being sidelined on May 29, 1985 at Ashland, Wisconsin due to the lack of ore cargoes the **INDIANA HARBOR** remained in lay-up at that port until she re-entered service on May 8th of the following year. Her return to service would not be without incident as high winds caused the **INDIANA HARBOR** to strike some loading chutes on the ore loading dock while departing, knocking down around 30-feet of her fence railing.

On September 9, 1993, while on Lake Michigan bound for Two Harbors the **INDIANA HARBOR** suffered heavy hull damages after running into the Lansing Shoal Lighthouse. The incident occurred just after the **INDIANA HARBOR** had departed Sturgeon Bay following the completion of a 5-year survey. During this accident the **INDIANA HARBOR** had a 50 square foot section of her hull plating

*Two generations of Great Lakes freighters pass. On the left is the **EDWARD L. RYERSON** which was built in 1960, was one of the last US flagged ships to be constructed with cabins both fore and aft, while the **INDIANA HARBOR** represents the standard thousand-foot vessel built between the early 1970s and 80s. Although less than twenty years separate the construction of these two ships, the **INDIANA HARBOR** can carry payloads over twice as large as those the **RYERSON** is capable of handling. This is despite the fact that the **EDWARD L. RYERSON** was designed with the maximum dimensions allowed for operation on the Great Lakes at the time of her construction.*

ripped open, requiring an immediate return trip to Sturgeon Bay for repairs. Repairs were to prove costly with the **INDIANA HARBOR**'s repair bill being reported to be valued at $1.9 million dollars, while the lighthouse suffered a loss estimated at $112,000. The **INDIANA HARBOR**'s stay at the shipyard lasted until October 22, 1993 when she finally re-entered service in the taconite trade.

Shortly after the **ST. CLAIR** (2) departed Superior, Wisconsin with a load of coal on May 20, 2001 it was discovered that water was being taken aboard through a hole in her starboard hull. This caused the 770-foot ship to return to the Twin Ports, tying up at Duluth, Minnesota. The following day, the **INDIANA HARBOR** came alongside the **ST. CLAIR** (2) to receive the cargo from the damaged ship. After unloading her payload of coal into the thousand-footer, the **ST. CLAIR** (2) went to nearby Fraser Shipyards for repairs.

While attempting to enter the harbor at Muskegon, Michigan on August 22, 2007, the **INDIANA HARBOR** ran aground in Lake Michigan. After being stranded for around 4 hours, the crew of the thousand-footer was able free the vessel enabling it to continue into Muskegon's harbor to unload her cargo of coal. On May 17, 2009, the **INDIANA HARBOR** made a rare trip up the St. Marys River with a coal cargo while making her way towards the Twin Ports. This was caused when the **INDIANA HARBOR** suffered a broken conveyor belt in her unloading system while discharging coal at Detroit Edison's St. Clair Power Plant at St. Clair, Michigan a few days previously. When the conveyor belt had broken, the **INDIANA HARBOR** had only unloaded around 1/3 of her cargo, with the remaining being carried aboard on her upbound trip for repairs.

During the winter lay-up period between the 2009 and 2010 shipping seasons the **INDIANA HARBOR** received a new set of power plants at Superior, Wisconsin. This involved the installation of two new diesel powered Caterpillar engines to generate the **INDIANA HARBOR**'s electrical needs. This upgrade replaced the ship's original generators with units which are more fuel efficient while also producing a lower emission footprint. Also receiving a similar modernization during the same timeframe was the **H. LEE WHITE (2)** which had her work done at Sturgeon Bay.

The **INDIANA HARBOR** has a mid-summer draft of 34-feet which allows a maximum payload of 78,850 tons of taconite to be transported. This ship is equipped with both bow and stern thrusters, enabling her to maneuver safely in waterways considered to be constricted for ships of her size. The **INDIANA HARBOR** has the dimensions of a standard thousand-footer built by the Bay Shipbuilding Corporation with a length of 1,000-feet, a beam of 105-feet, and a 56-foot depth. The **INDIANA HARBOR** is powered by four General Motors Electro-Motive Division 20-645-E7 diesel engines producing a total of 14,400 brake horsepower. This ship has a rated top speed of 16-miles per hour on the open lake and is driven by a pair of controllable pitch propellers.

As of the 2010 shipping season the **INDIANA HARBOR** remains active in the movement of taconite and coal from the upper lakes to the ports on the lower lakes. This ship was the second, and thus far last, thousand-footer built for the American Steamship fleet. However, she is now only one of six thousand-footers operated by the American Steamship Company, the others being the **WALTER J. McCARTHY, JR.**, **AMERICAN INTEGRITY**, **AMERICAN CENTURY**, **AMERICAN SPIRIT**, and the **BURNS HARBOR**. Of these, only the **McCARTHY** was built new for American Steamship when it entered service as the **BELLE RIVER** in 1977, while the others were acquired later in their careers after serving in other fleets.

EDGAR B. SPEER

While the **EDWIN H. GOTT** was being built at Sturgeon Bay, Wisconsin, the United States Steel Corporation was having a similar thousand-footer constructed by the American Ship Building Company. This ship was built in two separate pieces, with the forward section being fabricated at American Ship Building's Toledo, Ohio yard which was towed to Lorain, Ohio to be joined to the stern section. Despite being built at two separate facilities, this ship was given one hull number (Hull #908) by its builders. Work had begun on this ship during the first half of 1977 but its launching was delayed until the spring of 1980 due to a labor dispute at American Ship Building.

On May 8, 1980 this ship was launched at Lorain, with its christening as the **EDGAR B. SPEER** taking place a month later on June 4th. Following the completion of its sea trials during August, the **EDGAR B. SPEER** departed Lorain on September 20, 1980 bound for Two Harbors, Minnesota to load its first cargo of taconite destined for use in her owner's steel making operations.

This ship is very similar in appearance to the **EDWIN H. GOTT**, and like that vessel it was fitted with a transverse shuttle boom when it was constructed. With a length of 1,004-feet, a beam of 105-feet, and a 56-foot depth the **EDGAR B. SPEER** also has identical dimensions to US Steel's first operational thousand-footer. Both of these vessels represented a new era in US flagged Great Lakes shipping which had witnessed a class of ships being built for maximum efficiency with little attention being paid to traditional freshwater ship design. The days of building ships with stylish curves and cabins placed both forward and aft had passed by and were replaced by the building of ships with square lines and cabins placed only at the stern.

As was the case with the **EDWIN H. GOTT**, the **EDGAR B. SPEER** was also designed with winter operations in mind. However, by the time that the **EDGAR B. SPEER** entered service the concept of a year-round navigation season on the Great Lakes had been generally abandoned. While the 12-month season had been proven to be technically achievable, it had come at a heavy cost with ships participating in such operations being damaged on a regular basis. Also occurring during the early 1980s was a significant drop in the demand for the movement of iron ore on the Great Lakes as the domestic steel industry underwent a serious recession. With such economic conditions, many operators of fleets on the Great Lakes suddenly found themselves having difficulties in keeping their vessels employed during the regular season, much less being able to keep them employed through the winter months.

While all of the US flagged fleets on the Great Lakes would experience some difficult times during the 1980s, perhaps none suffered as heavily as the Great Lakes Fleet. In 1973 this fleet had 43 active vessels on the inland seas while just over a decade later, in 1984, this firm would actively employ only 10 ships while the remainder of their pool of vessels remained idle at various points around the lakes. Many of these ships would never return to service with most being scrapped by the end of the 1980s. So severe was the economic downturn that even the efficient **EDGAR B. SPEER** experienced some extended periods of idleness during this decade.

With a total of 39 ships in the fleet at the beginning of the 1980 season and only 12 remaining at the beginning of the 1990s, the downsizing of the Great Lakes Fleet during the decade of the 1980s was dramatic. This was caused in part by the fleet modernization program that the United States Steel

Corporation undertook during the 1970s which saw the construction of three new ships, and the lengthening of four others. Also contributing to the phasing out of older and less efficient vessels was the increasing reliance upon self-unloading ships in the ore trade and the general downsizing of the domestic steel industry as a whole.

While in lay-up at Sturgeon Bay, Wisconsin on December 2, 1985, the **EDGAR B. SPEER** along with Bethlehem Steel's **STEWART J. CORT** tore loose from their moorings during a windstorm. During this minor incident neither of these vessels reported any damages. In 1986, the United States Steel Corporation experienced a labor strike effecting their steel making operations. This caused the laying up of most of the Great Lakes Fleet, with the **EDGAR B. SPEER** being idled at Duluth, Minnesota by early August of that year. This period of inactivity lasted until May 21, 1987 when the **EDGAR B. SPEER** loaded taconite at Duluth bound for delivery to Gary, Indiana following the end of the labor dispute.

During the 1987 shipping season, the **EDGAR B. SPEER** was utilized to carry taconite to the United States Steel plant at Lorain, Ohio, where she arrived for the first time on November 27, 1987. Since this ship is much too large to make the trip up the Black River to unload at that facility's dock, an alternative method of delivering the taconite had to be formulated. A solution to this problem was found in off loading the **SPEER**'s cargo into the smaller **PHILIP R. CLARKE**, which would then make the run up the river to unload. Since the **CLARKE**'s capacity was much smaller than that of the **EDGAR B. SPEER** it was required to have the steamer make three trips before the thousand-footer was completely unloaded.

During the summer of 1988 control of the Great Lakes Fleet was transferred to Blackstone Capital

*The extreme breadth of the **EDGAR B. SPEER** is apparent as this ship makes her way back up the lakes for another load of taconite. Other than the addition of the black and gray stripes on her bow, the appearance of this ship has changed little since it entered service in 1980.*

*All three of the ships built for the United States Steel Corporation during the 1970s were fitted with unloading systems incorporating a transverse shuttle conveyor rather than conventional unloading booms of tubular construction. The **EDGAR B. SPEER**, and the **ROGER BLOUGH** retain their original unloading apparatuses, while the **EDWIN H. GOTT** received a rebuild in 1995 which saw the fitting a standard boom. In this picture, the shuttle boom can be seen fitted just forward of the **EDGAR B. SPEER**'s superstructure. When discharging her cargoes, such an arrangement restricts this ship to unloading at docks fitted with a receiving hopper system.*

Partners as the United States Steel Corporation sold its majority stake in the fleet, along with its other transportation properties. By the 1990 shipping season the ships in the Great Lakes Fleet received a new paint scheme to reflect the change in ownership. This change included the placement of a pair of black and gray stripes on the **EDGAR B. SPEER**'s bow. Although the Great Lakes Fleet was now an independent organization it still remained heavily committed to supplying the United States Steel Corporation with its material movement requirements on the Great Lakes.

In January of 2001, the **EDGAR B. SPEER** received a safety management certification from the American Bureau of Shipping, thus becoming the first US flagged freighter on the Great Lakes to receive such an endorsement. When the **ARTHUR M. ANDERSON** became disabled in the Straits of Mackinac on March 24, 2001 the **EDGAR B. SPEER** was tasked to tow the stricken steamer to the Bay Shipbuilding yard the following day. This tow proceeded without incident with the two ships arriving off of Sturgeon Bay on March 26th where they were met by the tugs **JIMMY L.** and **MARY PAGE HANNAH** which towed the **ANDERSON** into the shipyard to receive the necessary repairs.

While stuck in ice during its attempt to transit the Straits of Mackinac on April 7, 2003, the **EDGAR B. SPEER** went aground. The thousand-footer remained aground until the following morning when it was pulled free by the tug **RELIANCE**, with no significant damage being reported as having been caused by the stranding. Later that season, on December 3, 2003, the **EDGAR B. SPEER** lost one of its twin rudders in the St. Marys River near Lime Island. After going to anchor for a brief period, the **EDGAR B. SPEER** proceeded to Sturgeon Bay for the fitting of a replacement rudder.

In October of 2003 it was announced that the Great Lakes Fleet was being purchased from the Blackstone Group by Canadian National (CN). Following the sale, which was finalized in May of 2004, the operation of the Great Lakes Fleet was assumed by Key Lakes Incorporated, a subsidiary of Keystone Shipping.

On January 18, 2004 the downbound **EDGAR B. SPEER** became stuck in the Rock Cut due to a heavy build-up of ice. She remained stranded at this location for three days before being released on January 21st with the assistance of the tugs **MISSOURI, RELIANCE, JOSEPH H. THOMPSON, JR.,** and the **JOYCE L. VAN ENKEVORT**. Although no appreciable damage was reported to be suffered by the **EDGAR B. SPEER**, her becoming stuck delayed a number of vessels on their downbound trips through the icy St. Marys River.

The loss of a rudder would once again strike a ship operating in the Great Lakes Fleet when the **ROGER BLOUGH** lost her rudder on August 5, 2006 while downbound on the St. Marys River near Lime Island. Following the incident, the **BLOUGH** was forced to anchor, remaining there until August 8th when the **EDGAR B. SPEER** arrived to tow the disabled vessel to Gary, Indiana. The pair finally arrived at that location three days later, following an uneventful journey down Lake Michigan in a side by side manner. After unloading her cargo of taconite, the **ROGER BLOUGH** was taken to Sturgeon Bay for repairs.

The **EDGAR B. SPEER**'s carrying capacity is rated at a maximum of 73,700 tons which is offloaded by a shuttle boom capable of reaching a point of up to 52-feet to either the ship's port or starboard side to deposit cargo directly into a shore side hopper. Unlike the **EDWIN H. GOTT**, the **EDGAR B. SPEER** has not been refitted with a conventional boom during its career thus far. This has limited this vessel to operating solely in the transportation of ore from the upper lakes into the ports of Gary, Indiana and Conneaut, Ohio. In common with the **GOTT**, this ship does have smaller than normal hatches through which her cargoes are loaded. Each of the **EDGAR B. SPEER**'s hatches measures 28 feet long and 11 feet wide.

The **EDGAR B. SPEER** is equipped with a pair Pielstick 18PC2-3V-400 diesel engines generating a combined 19,260 brake horsepower. This thousand-footer is pushed through the water by two controllable-pitch propellers and has a rated speed of 17 miles per hour.

As of the 2010 shipping season the **EDGAR B. SPEER** continues to provide its owners with steadfast service in the transportation of taconite on the Great Lakes. This ship became the final vessel to be built for the United States Steel Corporation for service on the Great Lakes, bringing to a close an era of ship construction which began in 1905.

*The **EDGAR B. SPEER** was the final vessel constructed for United States Steel's Great Lakes Fleet. This ship was built to strictly haul taconite, a duty which she performs to this day. The **EDGAR B. SPEER** is shown downbound at St. Clair, Michigan on November 17, 2007 with a load of ore for delivery to Conneaut, Ohio.*

BURNS HARBOR

During the 1960s, the Bethlehem Steel Corporation embarked upon building a major steel making facility thirty miles southeast of Chicago at Burns Harbor, Indiana. This had followed several years of efforts by local officials to create a deep water port at the location, formerly know as Burn's Ditch, which had proved to be a lengthy process beginning during the 1930s. The construction of Bethlehem's steel mill had began during 1962, and would cause a major increase in the demand for seasonal tonnage movement by the ships of the giant steel maker's Great Lakes Steamship Division once it was declared operational. To address this issue, plans were formulated by company officials to begin a fleet renewal program beginning during the late 1960s which would lead to the construction of three thousand-foot vessels by the 1980 season.

On September 9, 1969, the steamer **STEELTON** (3) arrived off the entrance to Burns Harbor with what was intended to be the first cargo of ore for Bethlehem's fully integrated steel mill. However, heavy weather conditions present in lower Lake Michigan that day prevented the 621-foot steamer from entering the new harbor, causing her cargo to be diverted to South Chicago instead. Finally on September 11, 1969, the Bethlehem steamer **LEHIGH** (3) arrived at Burns Harbor to unload 15,700 tons of taconite which had been loaded at Taconite Harbor, Minnesota.

As mentioned earlier, the decade of the 1970s proved to be a period of significant growth for Bethlehem Steel's Great Lakes Steamship Division. In 1972, this fleet placed the first thousand-footer on the Great Lakes into service when the **STEWART J. CORT** was commissioned. This was followed in 1978 by the construction of the **LEWIS WILSON FOY**. Also taking place during this timeframe was the lengthening of the **ARTHUR B. HOMER** from 730-feet to 826-feet in 1976, and the conversion of the **SPARROWS POINT** from a straight deck bulk carrier to a self-unloader in 1980.

The last new vessel to be constructed for the Bethlehem fleet would be the building of the eleventh thousand-foot vessel to enter active service on the Great Lakes. The keel for this ship was laid on April 16, 1979 by the Bay Shipbuilding Corporation at Sturgeon Bay, Wisconsin. Construction on this ship, known initially as Hull #720, continued at a steady rate with her launching taking place on October 28, 1979, a little over six months since her construction began.

While still under construction on March 16, 1980, a small fire started underneath this ship's cargo hold which damaged a section of one of her unloading belts. This blaze began when some debris from the vessel's construction was ignited and singed around five feet of conveyor belt. On May 24, 1980, this ship was christened as the **BURNS HARBOR**, becoming the last ship to be added to the Bethlehem fleet. During July, this ship underwent her sea trials on Lake Michigan in anticipation of entering service in ore trade on the inland seas.

In a portent of the shape of things to come for the steel industry during the decade of the 1980s, the maiden voyage of the **BURNS HARBOR** was delayed following its sea trials due to the lack of demand for the movement of ore. After sitting idle for two months, the **BURNS HARBOR** finally departed Sturgeon Bay on September 28, 1980 bound for Superior, Wisconsin to load taconite destined for delivery to the steel mill after which it had been named. The maiden trip of the **BURNS HARBOR** followed the initial voyage of United States Steel's **EDGAR B. SPEER** by eight days. This marked the closest dates in which two ships of the thousand-foot class entered service while this class was being built during the nine year period between 1972 and 1981.

Being built at the same yard and to the same general design, the **BURNS HARBOR** was very similar in many respects to Bethlehem's **LEWIS WILSON FOY**. One of the most notable differences between the **BURNS HARBOR** and her other sisters built at Sturgeon Bay was the addition of an extra level of cabins, giving her a noticeably higher deckhouse. As was the case with the **LEWIS WILSON FOY**, this ship would be primarily engaged in the movement of iron ore originating on Lake Superior to be delivered to Burns Harbor, with an occasional trip to Lake Erie with ore for Bethlehem's steel plant at Lackawanna, New York. On one foray away from her usual haunts on Lake Michigan, the **BURNS HARBOR** is recorded as having unloaded a cargo of ore at the Great Lakes Steel plant on Zug Island, near Detroit, on May 10, 1983.

During the early 1980s, it was common for the **BURNS HARBOR** to lay-up for the winter at Erie, Pennsylvania. On December 29, 1983, this ship arrived at Erie to lay-up for the winter following being stuck in heavy ice on Lake Erie for five days. After spending the winter at the Pennsylvania port, the **BURNS HARBOR** departed on April 7, 1984 only to run into problems with her bow thrusters, prompting a return trip to Erie for repairs. Following the completion of the necessary corrections, the **BURNS HARBOR** finally departed on April 13, 1984 to begin her season.

The **BURNS HARBOR** set a Great Lakes cargo record on July 26, 1985 when she loaded 68,608 tons of ore at Escanaba, Michigan. This record cargo was destined for delivery to Indiana Harbor, and was later eclipsed by a fleet mate, the **LEWIS WILSON FOY,** when it loaded 72,351 tons of ore at Escanaba on November 26, 1986.

During early season runs it is somewhat common for Great Lakes ships to suffer minor hull damages

*The **BURNS HARBOR** is upbound on the St. Clair River during the 1994 shipping season. This ship was built with an extra level of cabins, giving her superstructure a noticeably taller appearance than those installed on her sister ships built by the Bay Shipbuilding Corporation.*

*The **BURNS HARBOR** is shown during a rare trip down the St. Clair River on April 6, 2008. This ship came into the American Steamship Company fleet during the 2005 season and is seen in her current colors.*

during their initial voyages as the lakes are still covered by large fields of ice. One such example occurred on April 3, 1994 when the **BURNS HARBOR** suffered ice damage in the Straits of Mackinac after departing from winter lay-up from Milwaukee, Wisconsin. The resulting damage was isolated to the thousand-footer's bow plating, just below the waterline. After taking on extra ballast in order to raise the damaged plating above the surface of the water, the **BURNS HARBOR** returned to Milwaukee for repairs.

In August of 1996, the **BURNS HARBOR** set a cargo record for iron ore originating from a Lake Superior port when she loaded 64,435 gross tons of taconite at Superior, Wisconsin. Two years later, on December 17, 1998, this ship made a rare trip into the Algoma Steel mill at Sault Ste. Marie, Ontario. During this unique voyage, this ship carried 49,000 tons of taconite to the steel making facility which had been loaded at Superior.

On December 30, 1999, the **BURNS HARBOR** received bottom damages while transiting Lake Michigan when it struck bottom at Grays Reef. Damages were relatively minor, but serious enough to cause the thousand-footer to proceed to Sturgeon Bay for winter lay-up and repairs.

Following a period of financial decline, the Bethlehem Steel Corporation filed for bankruptcy protection on October 15, 2001. This signified the beginning of the last days of a steel manufacturer which at one time was the second largest in the United States, being surpassed only by the giant United States Steel Corporation. During the early months of 2003, the International Steel Group made an offer to acquire Bethlehem Steel's assets for $1.5 billion. This transaction was later approved by the Federal Bankruptcy Court in April of that year.

As they were part of the sale agreement with the International Steel Group, both the **BURNS HARBOR** and the **STEWART J. CORT** were given new stack markings prior to the beginning of the 2004 shipping season signifying the dissolution of the Bethlehem Steel Corporation on December 31, 2003. The new stack markings consisted of an overall white stack with a black band at its top, with the

*A close up view of the stern cabins of the **BURNS HARBOR** show their arrangement that is generally in common with the other thousand-footers built at Sturgeon Bay, while at the same time illustrating its differences. The incorporation of an extra deck gives this ship's superstructure a more rectangular appearance, while the **BURNS HARBOR**'s stacks are also not as tall as those installed on her other sister ships.*

letters ISG, signifying the new owning company, and a stylized globe logo being placed upon the white stack.

In October of 2004, the International Steel Group was part of a massive merger which also included Ispat Steel, and the LNM Group to create Mittal Steel. This corporate restructuring, which was coordinated by European steel magnate Lakshmi Mittal, caused an immediate quandary concerning the operation of both of International Steel Group's former thousand-footers, the **BURNS HARBOR** and **STEWART J. CORT**, on domestic trade routes. This situation was the result of requirements stipulated by the Jones Act of 1920 which stated that all ships operating between US ports must be American owned. These difficulties were overcome in June of 2005 when the **BURNS HARBOR** was sold to the American Steamship Company.

Since becoming part of the American Steamship Company this ship has remained on its regular trade route between Superior and Burns Harbor. With the exception of the **EDWIN H. GOTT**, the **BURNS HARBOR** has a carrying capacity identical to the other thousand-foot ships built by the Bay Shipbuilding Corporation, this being a maximum capacity of 78,850 tons of ore. Cargo is offloaded with the use of conventional 250-foot unloading boom which is mounted on the face of the after cabins. This boom is able to swing up to 92-degrees to either side of the **BURNS HARBOR**'s centerline to deposit cargo either on a dock or a hopper.

The **BURNS HARBOR** has a length of 1,000-feet, a beam of 105-feet, and a depth of 56-feet. This ship's mid-summer draft is 34-feet. This ship has a powerplant arrangement consisting of four 3,600 horsepower General Motors Electro-Motive Division diesel engines. With a combined rating of 14,400 brake horsepower, these engines allow the **BURNS HARBOR** to reach a maximum speed just in excess of 18 miles per hour. Ships operating on the Great Lakes are expected to maneuver within constricted waterways as part of their normal operational pattern. To facilitate its flexibility while operating in such environments, the **BURNS HARBOR** is fitted with both bow and stern thrusters.

As of the 2010 season, the **BURNS HARBOR** remains active in the movement of iron ore from the upper lakes into Lake Michigan. Since being acquired by the American Steamship Company she has been repainted in their fleet colors, but has not been renamed. Thirty years after its construction, along with serving three different operators, the **BURNS HARBOR** remains hard at work carrying ore into Burns Harbor, Indiana, fulfilling the role for which it was originally built.

*The morning of May 11, 2010 finds the **BURNS HARBOR** at Sault Ste. Marie, Michigan awaiting passage through the Poe Lock. During the shipping season this thousand-footer will pass through this area numerous times as she plies her usual trade route carrying ore from Lake Superior to Burns Harbor, Indiana. On this particular occasion, she was delayed at the Soo Locks due to low water levels on the St. Marys River caused by several days of high winds. Most other passages are uneventful.*

WILLIAM J. DE LANCEY

In February of 1978, the Interlake Steamship Company and the Republic Steel Corporation signed a 25 year ore hauling contract. This agreement, which was to be fully implemented by 1981, caused many changes in the Interlake fleet including the conversion of the **ELTON HOYT 2nd** (2) from a straight deck bulk carrier into a self-unloader as well as the construction of a third thousand-foot vessel.

As was the case with this fleet's two previous superships, the **JAMES R. BARKER** and **MESABI MINER**, the American Ship Building Company was contracted to build the new ship. While similar in appearance and design to Interlake's thousand-footers preceding her, the new vessel would be slightly longer at 1,013-feet 6-inches. This extra length made this ship the longest ship ever built for service on the Great Lakes, a title that she retains to this day.

This ship was built in two sections with the bow segment being built at American Ship Building's Toledo, Ohio shipyard while the stern section was fabricated at Lorain, Ohio. After its launching at Toledo, the forward section of this ship was towed to Lorain where it was attached to the stern section. On February 4, 1981, this ship was float-launched at Lorain with its final fitting out taking place over the next several months.

On Saturday, April 25, 1981, representatives from Interlake Steamship, Picklands Mather & Co., Republic Steel, and American Ship Building gathered for the christening of the new ship. In recognition of the importance of the Republic Steel contract to the Interlake fleet this ship was named **WILLIAM J. DE LANCEY** to honor the steel maker's current chairman at the time. Following the christening ceremony, tours of the new vessel were given to employees of the four firms involved in the construction of the **DE LANCEY**, with the general public being allowed to board the ship for similar tours the following day. In the space of the two days it was estimated that over 20,000 people had toured the new supership.

The **WILLIAM J. DE LANCEY** became the last ship to be built by the American Ship Building Company, concluding that firm's long history of shipbuilding. This ship began its maiden voyage when it departed the shipyard on May 10, 1981 bound for Silver Bay, Wisconsin where it loaded 55,944 gross tons of taconite to be delivered to Lorain. The **DE LANCEY** was the second to last thousand-footer to enter service, followed only by the **COLUMBIA STAR** which began her maiden voyage 20 days later.

In 1980, the Republic Steel Corporation completed the construction of a ore pellet transshipment terminal at Lorain to supply its steel manufacturing centers located nearby Cleveland. This facility was necessary due to the fact that Republic's mills were along the twisting Cuyahoga River, which were inaccessible to ships with dimensions much greater than 634-feet in length. Since the regular use of such sized ships to transport ore from Lake Superior would be uneconomical in an era of thousand-foot vessels, a cost-effective solution had to be found. The answer was to construct an ore terminal at Lorain to receive taconite brought down the lakes by thousand-foot vessels which would in turn be reloaded into an army of smaller ships which could transport the ore up the tight confines of the Cuyahoga River and discharge it directly at Republic's steel mills. So important was this process for the US flagged fleet, that the American Steamship Company built a new vessel, the **AMERICAN REPUBLIC**, in 1981

*The **WILLIAM J. DE LANCEY** is downbound on the St. Clair River during the summer of 1989, the last season she carried that name. While this ship was in winter lay-up between the 1989 and 1990 seasons she was renamed **PAUL R. TREGURTHA**.*

*The **PAUL R. TREGURTHA** is shown discharging coal at the DTE Energy dock at St. Clair, Michigan. Originally constructed to principally carry taconite, this ship has been heavily dedicated to the movement of coal since the mid-1980s.*

incorporating several unique features which were specifically designed to facilitate the hauling of taconite between the Lorain transshipment facility and Republic Steel's docks.

Being the longest ship on the Great Lakes it is not surprising that this ship is noted as having set two cargo records for the hauling of taconite on Lake Michigan during her second season of operation. The first occurred on July 30, 1982 when this ship was loaded with 62,701 gross tons of ore at Escanaba, Michigan for delivery to Indiana Harbor, Indiana. A second occurred the following month, on August 7, 1982 when the **WILLIAM J. DE LANCEY** loaded another record at Escanaba, this time a 63,007 gross ton payload, also destined for Indiana Harbor.

The Lorain pellet terminal was a common destination for this ship during her early years of operation, although another significant contract being awarded to the Interlake Steamship Company would later witness the **WILLIAM J. DE LANCEY** becoming heavily utilized in the coal trade. At the beginning of the 1984 shipping season this ship was put to work carrying western coal from Superior, Wisconsin to Detroit Edison's two power plants located south of St. Clair, Michigan. At the time, Detroit Edison was placing the finishing touches on its then new Belle River power plant which sits adjacent to its St. Clair facility. The new plant, which was to going into operation during the summer of that year, had been under construction for several years and would dramatically increase the seasonal demand for coal delivery to that location.

The acquisition of the long-term agreement with Detroit Edison to haul 1.5 million tons of coal in 1984 and 3 million beginning the following year was of major importance for Interlake as the demand for ore plummeted during the early 1980s due to a severe recession taking place in the steel industry. The tonnage commitments provided by the coal hauling agreement during this time period surely allowed managers at Interlake to keep many of their ships in operation during that troubled decade which would have been unlikely without the Detroit Edison contract. Despite this, several of this fleet's ships would find themselves being idled for protracted periods of time during the 1980s.

The 1985 and 1986 shipping seasons would be interesting for the **WILLIAM J. DE LANCEY** as she was involved in a number of incidents, all of which were to be minor in nature. On April 21, 1985, this thousand-footer grounded briefly in Duluth's harbor near the Aerial Lift Bridge. Shortly after the incident, the **DE LANCEY** was able to resume her voyage with no damage being reported.

As Canada Steamship Lines' **MURRAY BAY** (3) was approaching Duluth, Minnesota on August 6, 1986 she nearly collided with the outbound **WILLIAM J. DE LANCEY**. Although the two ships did not come into contact with one another, they did come within 30-feet of a collision. An investigation into the incident found that high winds had caused the near accident.

While upbound in lower Lake Huron on October 27, 1986, a broken fuel line aboard the **JAMES R. BARKER** ignited a fire which disabled the vessel, causing her to go to anchor just north of Port Huron, Michigan. Two days later, the **WILLIAM J. DE LANCEY** arrived alongside the **BARKER** and began towing her in a side-by-side fashion to Sturgeon Bay, Wisconsin for repairs. After a lengthy tow, the two thousand footers finally arrived at their destination on November 2, 1986.

After loading coal at the Midwest Energy Terminal in Superior, Wisconsin on November 16, 1986 the **WILLIAM J. DE LANCEY** ran aground in St. Louis Bay. Initially it was planned to offload some of the **DE LANCEY**'s cargo into fleet mate **CHARLES M. BEEGHLY**. However, this plan was not necessary as an unexpected 3-inch rise in the water level of the harbor allowed the thousand-footer to float free from her perch before any cargo was transferred. No damage was reported as having been suffered by the **WILLIAM J. DE LANCEY** as a result of this occurrence.

In April of 1988, the **WILLAM J. DE LANCEY** delivered the first shipment of western coal to the

*The **PAUL R. TREGURTHA** passes under the twin spans of the Blue Water Bridge, which crosses the St. Clair River between Port Huron, Michigan and Point Edward, Ontario. This is the longest ship ever built for operation on the Great Lakes.*

B.C. Cobb Power Plant at Muskegon, Michigan. The use of this type of coal at that facility proved to be entirely successful with such deliveries by thousand-footers to that location remaining commonplace as of the 2010 shipping season.

Prior to the beginning of the 1990 shipping season this ship was renamed **PAUL R. TREGURTHA**. This had no effect upon the operation of this vessel as she remained committed to the movement of coal to supply Detroit Edison's needs while an occasional ore cargo was carried as the situation warranted it.

As the **PAUL R. TREGURTHA** was departing from the Twin Ports on June 30, 1990 she struck the north pier of the Duluth Ship Canal. This incident, which was blamed on strong currents, created a 2-foot crack in the thousand-footer's hull while the pier also received minor damage. After clearing the harbor, the **PAUL R. TREGURTHA** anchored in Lake Superior before returning to Duluth for repairs.

While this ship's troubles at the Twin Ports over the years have been relatively minor in nature, it is perhaps an incident that occurred on November 22, 1993 which had the potential to have catastrophic results had it not been for the quick actions of the **PAUL R. TREGURTHA**'s crew. On this date, the Duluth Aerial Lift Bridge was being raised to allow the **TREGURTHA** to depart Duluth Harbor when it became stuck in a partially raised position. Recognizing the danger, the crew of the **TREGURTHA** was able to bring their vessel to a stop in time to prevent the superstructure of the thousand-footer from striking the bridge, but not before the bow had passed below it. After backing out of the Duluth Ship Canal, the **TREGURTHA** proceeded to tie up at the Port Terminal as she was loaded too deep to use the Superior Entrance to depart the Twin Ports. The following morning, repairs were completed to the Aerial Bridge allowing the **PAUL R. TREGURTHA** to resume her trip to the lower lakes.

On December 21, 1999 this vessel grounded once again at the Twin Ports as she was attempting to depart using the Superior Entrance. When loaded with cargo, the draft of the **PAUL R. TREGURTHA** normally restricts her to using the Duluth Ship Canal while departing from Duluth and Superior's shared harbor. However, when this incident took place, the Duluth Aerial Lift Bridge was closed for repairs thus forcing all ships arriving and departing the Twin Ports to use the Superior Entrance. The **PAUL R. TREGURTHA** did not report any damage and was later able to float free from the bottom of the harbor after unloading a portion of her cargo into the **CANADIAN ENTERPRISE**.

While transiting the St. Marys River during heavy ice conditions on January 7, 2001, the **PAUL R. TREGURTHA** ran aground near Light 33. The location of the incident took place near the entrance to the Rock Cut and caused some flooding of the vessel's forepeak. After freeing itself, the **PAUL R. TREGURTHA** was allowed to proceed to St. Clair, Michigan to unload her cargo of coal before receiving repairs later that month at Bay Shipbuilding.

At the end of its 2009 season, the **PAUL R. TREGURTHA** laid up at Sturgeon Bay where it was to be repowered by the Bay Shipbuilding Corporation. After the removal of its original Pielstick 16PC-3V -400 engines in November 2009, two new MaK 6M43C diesel engines were installed. Each of these power plants is capable of producing 8,040 brake horsepower, thus giving the **PAUL R. TREGURTHA** a total of 16,080 horsepower. The new engines were installed during December of 2009 enabling this ship to resume service at the beginning of the following season when she departed the shipyard on April 8, 2010.

The **PAUL R. TREGURTHA** has an overall length of 1,013-feet 6-inches, a width of 105-feet, and a 56-foot depth. This provides the **TREGURTHA** the capability of carrying up to 68,000 gross tons of taconite or 71,250 net tons of coal on each trip. The **PAUL R. TREGURTHA** unloads her cargo via a 260-foot unloading boom located just in front of the ship's cabins at a spot 92-feet away from the stern of the ship. When loaded to its maximum capacity this ship has a draft of 30-feet 1-inch. The **PAUL R. TREGURTHA** is also equipped with a bow thruster to aid in maneuverability while in constricted areas or docking.

This ship has a cargo hold divided into 5 subsections which collectively have a total of 2,992,650 cubic feet of stowage space. This number reflects the highest such value of any of the thousand footers built by the American Ship Building Company. However, three others ships have cubic capacities greater than the **TREGURTHA** despite being shorter in length. These are American Steamship's **WALTER J. McCARTHY, JR., INDIANA HARBOR**, and **AMERICAN CENTURY** which were all constructed with cargo holds possessing 2,998,075 cubic feet of storage area.

As of the 2010 shipping season, the **PAUL R. TREGURTHA** continues to operate in the movement of coal and ore on the inland seas. With its repowering taking place between the 2009 and 2010 shipping seasons this ship should remain active on the Great Lakes for many years to come.

COLUMBIA STAR

In 1921, the Oglebay Norton Company purchased 11 ships from the Richardson fleet to create the Columbia Steamship Company. Despite being involved in the operation of numerous vessels for many years prior to the creation of this fleet, Oglebay Norton and its preceding corporate entities had not maintained a fleet on the Great Lakes in a practical sense up to that time. The beginnings of the Oglebay Norton Company can be traced back to 1851 when the ore brokering firm Hewitt & Tuttle was formed. This firm had been a pioneer in the tapping of iron ore reserves present around Lake Superior in Michigan and Minnesota. Hewitt & Tuttle were involved in the first shipment of iron ore from Lake Superior to Cleveland, Ohio in 1852. During this timeframe the shipment of ore from Lake Superior was a very expensive proposition as the St Marys Ship Canal had not yet been completed. This meant that ships were prohibited from passing between Lake Superior and Lake Huron due to the rapids at Sault Ste. Marie, Michigan. Therefore, cargo coming down from Lake Superior had to be unloaded above the rapids and then transported to a location further south on the St. Marys River to be reloaded into vessels which were at the Lake Huron level. This arrangement was very inefficient and created a very time consuming link in the chain of raw material movement from the northernmost of the five Great Lakes to customers on the lower lakes.

In 1855 Hewitt & Tuttle once again took part in a notable event in Great Lakes shipping history when it was involved in the first bulk shipment of iron ore from Lake Superior directly to the lower lakes. This occurred when the brig **COLUMBIA** departed from Marquette, Michigan on August 14, 1855 with 132 tons of iron ore aboard. The **COLUMBIA** would later deliver her cargo directly to Cleveland after passing through the new canal locks at Sault Ste. Marie which had opened earlier that year on June 18th. The 132 tons of ore that the **COLUMBIA** transported on this voyage were to pave the way for countless cargoes of ore which would follow from Lake Superior to unloading points on the lower lakes servicing the steel manufacturing industry.

By the 1880s, this firm had gone through several changes becoming Tuttle, Oglebay & Co. in 1884 with the arrival of Earl W. Oglebay. This arrangement would be short lived, however, as Earl W. Oglebay would later buy out the other members of the Tuttle family following the death of one of the company's principals in 1889. The following year, this firm was renamed Oglebay, Norton & Co. after David Z. Norton, a Cleveland banker, joined the organization.

Following its creation in 1921, the Columbia Steamship Company continued to expand its operations, later being renamed to the Columbia Transportation Company in 1935. During the early 1950s a strong demand for the movement of raw materials on the lakes combined with an overall aging fleet created the conditions which sparked a decade long increase in new ship construction for the US flagged fleet. During this decade the Columbia Transportation fleet would be expanded with the inclusion of the steamers **ARMCO** and **RESERVE** which both entered service in 1953. In 1958, these two ships were joined by the **EDMUND FITZGERALD** following Columbia's entry into a long term charter arrangement with that ship's owners, the Northwestern Mutual Life Insurance Company.

The 729-foot **EDMUND FITZGERALD** would remain the largest ship in the Columbia fleet until the acquisition of the **PIONEER CHALLENGER** from the Pioneer Steamship Company in 1962. This ship was promptly renamed **MIDDLETOWN** and had a length and depth just a few inches greater than that of the **EDMUND FITZGERALD**. Both the **MIDDLETOWN** and the **FITZGERALD** represented the largest ships allowed to operate on the Great Lakes prior to the opening of the new Poe Lock at Sault Ste. Marie in 1969.

The opening of the new Poe Lock enabled ship owners to lengthen some of their newer vessels. To this end, the **ARMCO** was lengthened from 647-feet to 767-feet in 1974 by the Fraser Shipyards at Superior, Wisconsin while the **RESERVE** underwent an identical lengthening the following year. While restricting these two steamers from venturing any further east than Lake Erie, these reconstructions were an ideal method to increase their efficiency in carrying bulk materials on their regular trade routes.

On November 10, 1975, the **EDMUND FITZGERALD** was lost on Lake Superior with all hands while downbound with taconite from Superior, Wisconsin. The sinking of the **FITZGERALD**, the cause of which is still debated to this day, represents the most modern major shipwreck on the Great Lakes involving a heavy loss of life.

On May 26, 1979, the **FRED R. WHITE, JR.** entered service for the Columbia Transportation fleet, thus becoming the first ship to be built for Oglebay Norton since the 1950s. With a length of 636-feet, a width of 68-feet, and a 40-foot depth, this ship was one of several similarly sized ships built for the US fleet during the 1970s which were optimized for operation in ports which had docks in constricted waterways such as those found at Cleveland, Ohio.

In September of 1979, the Oglebay Norton Company and the Bay Shipbuilding Corporation reached an agreement for the construction of a thousand-foot vessel. At the time, the Columbia Transportation

The **COLUMBIA STAR** is upbound on the St. Clair River just about to pass under the span of the original Blue Water Bridge during the 1992 shipping season. Ever since its construction, this ship has been a common sight passing the many communities located along the St. Clair River, locally referred to as the Blue Water Area..

*The **COLUMBIA STAR** is upbound near Marysville, Michigan on a summer morning during the 2000 shipping season. She has just off-loaded a cargo of western coal at the Detroit Edison dock in St. Clair, Michigan and is on her way back up the lakes for another such cargo consigned for the same destination.*

fleet had several of its ships engaged in the movement of ore from the upper lakes to the lower lakes. Much of this iron ore was loaded at Silver Bay, Wisconsin with Toledo, Ohio being a common unloading port. It was trade routes such as this that thousand-foot vessels were ideally suited for.

The keel for this ship was laid on March 3, 1980 with primary construction continuing until its launching later that same year on November 8th. Over the next several months this ship's construction was completed and on May 8, 1981 she was christened as the **COLUMBIA STAR**. After a few weeks of finishing touches, the **COLUMBIA STAR** departed Sturgeon Bay on May 30, 1981 on her maiden voyage to load 59,244 tons of taconite pellets at Silver Bay for delivery to Lorain, Ohio.

When the **COLUMBIA STAR** departed the shipyard she was noteworthy in that she was not only the last thousand-footer to enter service on the Great Lakes but also the last ship to be built for Oglebay Norton. In fact, the **COLUMBIA STAR** was also the last new self-powered ship to enter service for the US flagged Great Lakes fleet as of the 2010 shipping season.

The **COLUMBIA STAR** managed to set some cargo records during the early years of her career. On July 12, 1985 the **COLUMBIA STAR** is recorded as delivering the largest cargo of iron ore brought into Toledo, Ohio up to that time when she unloaded 64,068 gross tons of taconite. The following year, on July 2, 1986, this ship arrived at Escanaba, Michigan and loaded a record 70,001 gross tons of ore bound for delivery to Indiana Harbor, Indiana. This was made possible by the fact that this voyage took place entirely on Lake Michigan, therefore her depth was not restricted by the requirement of passing through any of the channels which connect the Great Lakes such as the St. Clair River.

At the beginning or ending of a shipping season it is common for ships to experience delays due to ice. This is especially true for thousand-foot vessels transiting the Poe Lock at Sault Ste. Marie, Michigan. One such instance occurred on April 17, 1988 when winds pushed large amounts of ice down from Lake Superior and into the upper St. Marys River where it caused the **COLUMBIA STAR** to take nearly six hours to successfully pass through the upper reaches of the river. Later that same year, on December 18, 1988, the **COLUMBIA STAR** ran into trouble at Sault Ste. Marie when a cable on a partially raised lock boom caught one of this ship's bridge wings, causing minor damage.

During the late 1980s the Columbia Transportation fleet began hauling western coal from Lake Superior down the lakes to Detroit Edison's power plants located in southern Michigan. After acquiring this contract, the **COLUMBIA STAR** became a common caller at Detroit Edison's St. Clair Michigan facility which has its unloading dock along the shores of the St. Clair River, just north of Marine City, at Recors Point. At the time, this trading pattern was also being served by thousand-foot vessels from the American Steamship and Interlake Steamship fleets. In 1991, this ship was joined on this route by a near sister ship, the **OGLEBAY NORTON**, which had been acquired as the **LEWIS WILSON FOY** from the Bethlehem Steel fleet.

While loading coal at the Superior Midwest Energy Terminal at Superior, Wisconsin on November 10, 1991 it was discovered that one of the **COLUMBIA STAR**'s ballast tanks had been holed. The loading was immediately stopped and 10,000 tons of her coal cargo was offloaded into American Steamship's **ST. CLAIR** (2) after which the **COLUMBIA STAR** shifted over to the Port Terminal in Duluth for an inspection before being cleared to continue loading.

As the **COLUMBIA STAR** departed Duluth on June 23, 1993, a sailboat was caught by the suction of the thousand-footer's propellers and dragged into Lake Superior. After the **COLUMBIA STAR** came to a stop it was found that while the incident significantly damaged the sailboat, it did not cause any injuries to its occupants.

Throughout the 1990s the **COLUMBIA STAR** was kept busy hauling ore and coal cargoes, with the

*On May 6, 2007, the **AMERICAN CENTURY** is downbound at Port Huron, Michigan in transitional colors reflecting the change in her ownership from the Oglebay Norton Company to the American Steamship Company during 2006. Since entering service in May of 1981 this ship has remained active in the transportation of coal and ore on the Great Lakes.*

78

coal run between Superior, Wisconsin and St. Clair, Michigan being commonplace. Voyages into Muskegon, Michigan with coal for the B.C. Cobb power plant was also a frequent destination for this ship along with her fleet mate **OGLEBAY NORTON**.

During the mid-1990s Oglebay Norton reorganized their shipping operations on the Great Lakes, eliminating their Columbia Transportation and Pringle Transit divisions to bring all of their ships into a single marine division within the corporation. The red stars marked with the letter "C" signifying the Columbia Transportation fleet were removed from the stacks of the ships in this fleet during the early 1990s leaving only a brown stack encircled by a yellow band at its mid-center. Following the creation of the Oglebay Norton Marine Transportation Division each of the ships in this fleet had new logos placed upon their stacks consisting of a stylized four pointed star with the letters "ON" placed upon its center symbolizing the Oglebay Norton Company. This same logo was also placed on each side of their ship's bows along with the text "OGLEBAY NORTON COMPANY" being painted in large block letters.

During the early 2000s, Oglebay Norton began to run into serious financial difficulties and by the 2003 shipping season many of their ships were idled due to a loss of available cargoes. On February 23, 2004 Oglebay Norton filed for bankruptcy protection after several years of financial decline. Following the decision to leave the Great Lakes shipping industry, Oglebay Norton began to sell its fleet of ships. In 2005, the **BUCKEYE** (3) was sold for conversion to a barge while early in the following year the **RESERVE** also left the fleet. On June 6, 2006, six ships were sold to the American Steamship Company for a reported $120 million US dollars. This transaction included the **COLUMBIA STAR**, **OGLEBAY NORTON**, **FRED R. WHITE, JR,**. **COURTNEY BURTON**, **MIDDLETOWN**, and the **ARMCO**.

*The **AMERICAN CENTURY** is shown on Lake Huron on May 2, 2010. She has by this time been fully re-painted in the standard colors of the American Steamship fleet. This ship was the last self-powered US flagged vessel to enter service on the Great Lakes.*

After becoming a member of the American Steamship fleet, the **COLUMBIA STAR** was renamed **AMERICAN CENTURY**. Following this transition the operation of this ship has been relatively unchanged as she remains actively engaged in the hauling of both ore and coal from the upper lakes to unloading points along the lower lakes.

The **AMERICAN CENTURY** is powered by four General Motors Electro-Motive Division 20-645-E7 diesel engines. With a combined 14,400 brake horsepower this powerplant arrangement gives this thousand-footer a top speed of 17-miles per hour, although she usually operates at a lower, more economical, cruising speed.

This ship has a maximum carrying capacity of 78,850 tons which is in common with the four other similar ships built by the Bay Shipbuilding Corporation, these being the **BELLE RIVER, LEWIS WILSON FOY, INDIANA HARBOR,** and **BURNS HARBOR**. A fifth thousand-foot vessel built by the same yard, the **EDWIN H. GOTT,** has some similarity to these vessels but was built to different design specification and has a 74,100 ton carrying capacity. Cargo is loaded aboard the **AMERICAN CENTURY** through 37 individual hatches placed on 24-foot centers and offloaded to shore via a 260-foot unloading boom. The cargo hold is divided into 7 separate sections and has a total of 2,998,075 cubic square feet of stowage space which allows for the capability of carrying up to 71,300 net tons of coal. The **AMERICAN CENTURY** is also equipped with both bow and stern thrusters which assist this ship in making the 180-degree turn in the St. Clair River necessary to arrive at the DTE Energy coal dock at St. Clair, Michigan to unload coal.

Built originally for the transportation of ore from Lake Superior to Toledo, Ohio this ship was later able to adapt to the changing needs of her original owners as they obtained sizable coal hauling contracts during the mid-1980s. This ship was by far the largest ship ever built for the Oglebay Norton Company which was finally dissolved in 2008 when its assets were acquired by Carmeuse Lime and Stone, a subsidiary of the Belgium based firm Carmeuse Group S.A..

The Future...

The arrival of thousand-foot vessels on the Great Lakes signified a significant advancement for the Great Lakes shipping industry. Even today, nearly forty years after the first of their kind entered service, they still represent the benchmark for the efficient movement of raw materials within the Great Lakes region. Simply put, there is no other available method which is more efficient to move the amount of cargo which can be loaded into one of these superships and transport it over the distances involved.

As ships of the thousand-foot class become increasingly aged they will either require upgrading or replacement. The most likely scenario which will occur over the next couple of decades will be the refurbishment of existing vessels rather than any new construction of superships. Since these ships have spent their entire lives on the Great Lakes, their hulls should remain sound for many years to come, although their propulsion systems will most likely require replacing as their engines become long in the tooth. In fact, the repowering of thousand-foot ships has already begun to take place with both the **PAUL R. TREGURTHA** and **EDWIN H. GOTT** receiving new diesel engine installations during the past two seasons.

Although the new Poe Lock enabled the US flagged fleet to modernize itself throughout the 1970s and into the early 1980s, it has also become its Achilles heel. This is due to the fact that this is the only lock at Sault Ste. Marie, Michigan which can handle ships measuring over 730-feet wide and 76-feet in width. Of the 48 US flagged vessels in the bulk material trades on the Great Lakes only 17 of them are able to pass through the MacArthur Lock, the next largest lock at the Soo.

Therefore, a prolonged shutdown of the Poe Lock due to mechanical failure or an accident would effectively stop the movement of raw materials to and from Lake Superior by the US flagged fleet. This would in essence send most of the superships into immediate lay-up although some would be able to continue trading by loading at Escanaba, Michigan, the only ore loading facility on the upper lakes located below the Soo Locks. Additional relief could also be found in allowing ships up to 767-feet in length to pass through the Mac Arthur Lock. Under special circumstances, this has been proven to be possible in the past and would allow the majority of the steamers lengthened during the 1970s to make the passage between Lakes Superior and Huron. However, in the final analysis, it is apparent that nearly 80 percent of the carrying capacity of the US flagged fleet would be directly impacted by the shutting down of the Poe Lock.

Confronted with this situation, US flagged shipping companies have campaigned for many years for the construction of a second lock at Sault Ste. Marie with dimensions in common with the Poe Lock. This sparked off a debate which carried on for three decades, and despite the US Congress approving the building of a new lock in 1986 no actual construction work would begin until nearly 25 years later.

On June 30, 2009, officials gathered at Sault Ste. Marie to participate in the official groundbreaking ceremonies signifying the beginning of the new lock's construction. At the time, this construction project was projected to cost nearly $600 million dollars and require up to 10 years to be completed. However, just one year later, in June of 2010, the construction of the new lock was placed on hold when the project did not receive funding in the current federal budget. How much effect this delay will have on the new lock's actual cost and date of completion has yet to be determined.

*The barge **GREAT LAKES TRADER** and its tug, the **JOYCE L. VAN ENKEVORT**, are downbound in Lake Huron on May 12, 2010. This barge arrived on the Great Lakes during the 2000 shipping season after being built in Mississippi. As such, it was the first new bulk freight vessel built for the US flagged fleet since 1981. Since entering service this tug-barge unit has been active in the ore, coal, and stone trades around the lakes.*

*A stern view of the **GREAT LAKES TRADER / JOYCE L. VAN ENKEVORT** combination illustrates the positioning of the tug at the stern of the barge. Although many believe that this type of vessel represents the future of US flagged shipping on the Great Lakes, the concept has yet to gain wide acceptance within the industry.*

When this lock is finally completed, at some point in the future, it will not usher in a new era of ship construction on the lakes in the manner that the opening of the Poe Lock signified in 1969. While the Poe Lock opened the possibility of constructing lake freighters to dimensions which had to that point only resided in the dreams of ship builders, the new lock is intended to simply double the capacity of the Soo Locks to handle the superships while at the same time providing a safeguard against a traffic stoppage in the event that the existing Poe Lock is put out of commission.

Shipping operations on the Great Lakes have always been directly tied to the economy. This is due to the fact that shipping fleets do not create their own demands, but rather provide a service for the cost-effective movement of raw materials in response to the requirements of manufacturers. Over the years, the Great Lakes shipping industry has weathered several economic storms, with one of the worst such periods occurring during the early 1980s. During that time period numerous ships were idled, many of which were eventually sold for scrap.

Perhaps, the most interesting facet of this decade was the scrapping of several ships which had been built during the 1950s. After serving for only 30 years, these ships were comparatively young by freshwater standards as most ships operating solely on the Great Lakes are expected to have service lives lasting at least 60-70 years. The scrapping of most of these younger vessels was directly correlated with the general downsizing of the domestic steel industry combined with the introduction of the thousand-footers, rebuilding of existing vessels, and the increased reliance on self-unloading technology in the ore trade.

During the last half of the 2008 shipping season, a global economic recession made an impact upon shipping operations on the Great Lakes when several ships were idled due to a lack of cargoes. These

*The steamer **RESERVE** is shown transiting the St. Clair River on July 22, 2007. This ship was built in 1953 for the Columbia Transportation fleet, a division of the Oglebay Norton Company. During the 1970s this ship was lengthened to 767-feet and later converted into a self-unloader in 1983. This ship remained in the Columbia fleet until being sold to Reserve Holdings, an affiliate of K&K Integrated Logistics, in 2006. A few weeks after this photograph was taken, this ship's conversion to a barge began at Menominee, Michigan.*

conditions persisted throughout the following year, with some recovery being experienced by the beginning of the 2010 season. This recession represented one of the most severe downturns in shipping since the 1980s, and it will most likely take several years for the shipping industry to fully recover. However, unlike what took place during the recession three decades earlier, there has been no wholesale scrapping of idled ships.

While at the current time there are no plans for the building of new self-powered ships for the US fleet, there are several who believe that the future of freshwater ship construction can be found in the barge **GREAT LAKES TRADER**. This self-unloading barge measures 740-feet long, 78-feet wide, and 45-feet deep. It was constructed in 2000 by the Halter Marine Group in Pearlington, Mississippi and brought to the Great Lakes through the St. Lawrence Seaway. It is paired with the tug **JOYCE L. VAN ENKEVORT** and has a maximum carrying capacity of 39,600 gross tons of iron ore. When these two vessels are paired their overall length is 845-feet, just 13-feet shorter than the **ROGER BLOUGH**.

The use of tug-barge combinations is not new to the Great Lakes shipping industry, nor are they unknown to the thousand-footer class as can be witnessed by the **PRESQUE ISLE** (2). Despite this, there has been some reluctance over the years within the US flagged fleet to construct new barge units to replace existing tonnage. Therefore, most of the barge units which have entered service have been converted from ships which had become obsolete as powered vessels.

Whether or not tug-barge combinations represent the next breed of superships on the Great Lakes has yet to be determined, although it is extremely unlikely that as long as there is a demand for raw material movement on the inland seas that there will come a day in which there are no self-powered ships on the Great Lakes.

*After the **RESERVE** was converted into a barge, it was renamed **JAMES L. KUBER** and paired with the tug **VICTORY**. The duo is shown here downbound on the St. Clair River at Marysville, Michigan on May 25, 2008. Interestingly, at the time this photograph was taken the name **RESERVE** remained painted on the **KUBER**'s hatch crane.*

Quick Reference Guide

JAMES R. BARKER-Built: 1976-American Ship Building Company, Lorain, Ohio. Dimensions: 1004' x 105' x 50'. Capacity: 63,300 gross tons. Operator (2011): Interlake Steamship Company. Official Number: 573682.

BELLE RIVER-Built: 1977-Bay Shipbuilding Corporation, Sturgeon Bay, Wisconsin. Renamed WALTER J. McCARTHY, JR. in 1990. Dimensions: 1000' x 105' x 56'. Capacity: 78,850 gross tons. Operator (2011): American Steamship Company. Official Number: 585952.

BURNS HARBOR-Built: 1980-Bay Shipbuilding Corporation, Sturgeon Bay, Wisconsin. Dimensions: 1000' x 105' x 56'. Capacity: 78,850 gross tons. Operator (2011): American Steamship Company. Official Number: 618479.

COLUMBIA STAR-Built: 1981-Bay Shipbuilding Corporation, Sturgeon Bay, Wisconsin. Dimensions: 1000' x 105' x 56'. Capacity: 78,850 gross tons. Renamed AMERICAN CENTURY in 2006. Operator (2011): American Steamship Company. Official Number: 635289.

STEWART J. CORT-Bow & stern built: 1970-Ingalls Shipbuilding Corporation, Pascagoula, Mississippi. Mid-section built: 1971-Erie Marine Incorporated, Erie, Pennsylvania. Final assembly completed at Erie Marine Incorporated in 1972. Dimensions: 1000' x 105' 49'. Capacity: 58,000 gross tons. Operator (2011): Interlake Steamship Company. Official Number: 532272.

WILLIAM J. DE LANCEY-Built: 1981-American Ship Building Company, Lorain, Ohio. Dimensions: 1,013' 6" x 105' x 56'. Capacity: 68,000 gross tons. Renamed PAUL R. TREGURTHA in 1990. Operator (2011): Interlake Steamship Company. Official Number: 631668.

LEWIS WILSON FOY-Built: 1978-Bay Shipbuilding Corporation, Sturgeon Bay, Wisconsin. Dimensions: 1000' x 105' 56'. Capacity: 78,850 gross tons. Renamed OGLEBAY NORTON in 1991. Renamed AMERICAN INTEGRITY in 2006. Operator (2011): American Steamship Company. Official Number: 592377.

EDWIN H. GOTT-Built: 1979-Bay Shipbuilding Corporation, Sturgeon Bay, Wisconsin. Dimensions: 1004' x 105' x 56'. Capacity: 74,100 gross tons. Operator (2011): Great Lakes Fleet, Incorporated. Official Number: 600648.

INDIANA HARBOR-Built: 1979-Bay Shipbuilding Corporation, Sturgeon Bay, Wisconsin. Dimensions: 1000' x 105' x 56'. Capacity: 78,850 gross tons. Operator (2011): American Steamship Company. Operator: 610401.

MESABI MINER-Built: 1977-American Steamship Company, Lorain, Ohio. Dimensions: 1004' x 105' x 50'. Capacity: 63,300 gross tons. Operator (2011): Interlake Steamship Company. Official Number: 581479.

PRESQUE ISLE (2)-Tug Built: 1973-Halter Marine Services Inc., New Orleans, Louisiana. Barge Built: (hull) 1973-Erie Marine Incorporated, Erie, Pennsylvania. (bow) 1972-Defoe Shipbuilding Company, Bay City, Michigan. Final assembly of barge completed at Erie Marine Incorporated. Dimensions of vessel in operational configuration: 1000' x 104' 7" x 46' 6". Capacity: 57,500 gross tons. Operator (2011): Great Lakes Fleet, Incorporated. Official Numbers: 553417 (barge) 553446 (tug).

EDGAR B. SPEER-Built: 1980-American Ship Building Company, Lorain, Ohio. Dimensions: 1004' x 105' x 56'. Capacity: 73,700 gross tons. Operator (2011): Great Lakes Fleet, Incorporated. Official Number: 621104.

GEORGE A. STINSON-Built: 1978-American Ship Building Company, Lorain, Ohio. Dimensions: 1004' x 105' x 50'. Capacity: 59,700 gross tons. Renamed AMERICAN SPIRIT in 2004. Operator (2011): American Steamship Company. Official Number: 595539.

APPENDIX

APPENDIX

THOUSAND-FOOT SHIPS ON THE GREAT LAKES

NAME	BUILT	LENGTH	WIDTH	DEPTH	CAPACITY	BUILDING SHIPYARD	Maiden Voyage	ORIGINAL OPERATOR
STEWART J. CORT*	1972	1,000'	105'	49'	58,000	Erie Marine Inc.	May 1, 1972	Bethlehem Steel Corporation
PRESQUE ISLE (2)**	1973	1,000'	104' 7"	46' 6"	57,500	Erie Marine Inc.***	December 16, 1973	Litton Great Lakes Corporation
JAMES R. BARKER	1976	1,004'	105'	50'	63,300	American Ship Building Company	August 8, 1976	Interlake Steamship Company
MESABI MINER	1977	1,004'	105'	50'	63,300	American Ship Building Company	June 7, 1977	Interlake Steamship Company
BELLE RIVER	1977	1,000'	105'	56'	78,850	Bay Shipbuilding Corporation	August 31, 1977	American Steamship Company
LEWIS WILSON FOY	1978	1,000'	105'	56'	78,850	Bay Shipbuilding Corporation	June 8, 1978	Bethlehem Steel Corporation
GEORGE A. STINSON	1978	1,004'	105'	50'	59,700	American Ship Building Company	October 14, 1978	National Steel Corporation
EDWIN H. GOTT	1979	1,004'	105'	56'	74,100	Bay Shipbuilding Corporation	February 16, 1979	United States Steel Great Lakes Fleet
INDIANA HARBOR	1979	1,000'	105'	56'	78,850	Bay Shipbuilding Corporation	August 29, 1979	American Steamship Company
EDGAR B. SPEER	1980	1,004'	105'	56'	73,700	American Ship Building Company	September 20, 1980	United States Steel Great Lakes Fleet
BURNS HARBOR	1980	1,000'	105'	56'	78,850	Bay Shipbuilding Corporation	September 28, 1980	Bethlehem Steel Corporation
WILLIAM J. DE LANCEY	1981	1,013' 6"	105'	56'	68,000	American Ship Building Company	May 10, 1981	Interlake Steamship Company
COLUMBIA STAR	1981	1,000'	105'	56'	78,850	Bay Shipbuilding Corporation	May 30, 1981	Columbia Transportation

Total Capacity: 911,850

*=Bow and Stern built at Ingalls Shipbuilding Corporation, Pascagoula, Mississippi. Joined to mid-section built at Erie Marine for final assembly.

**=Overall dimensions are given for the tug and barge combined in their operational configuration.

***=Barge was built by Erie Marine, joined with tug built at Halter Marine Services in New Orleans, Lousiana.

The above chart lists the 13 ships of the thousand-foot class in order of the date of their maiden voyages. As can be seen in the chart, beginning in 1977 and ending in 1981 thousand-foot ships were added to the US flagged fleet at a rate of 2 per year. Also easily discernible in this listing is the fact that after the STEWART J. CORT and PRESQUE ISLE (2) were completed at Erie Marine, all of the other thousand footers were built by either the American Ship Building Company or the Bay Shipbuilding Corporation.

89

APPENDIX

US FLAGGED SHIPS BUILT FOR THE BULK TRADE BETWEEN 1972 & 1981

Vessel	Built	Length	Width	Depth	Capacity	Original Owner
ROGER BLOUGH	1972	858'	105'	41' 6"	43,900	United States Steel Corporation
STEWART J. CORT	1972	1000'	105'	49'	58,000	Bethlehem Steel Corporation
CHARLES E. WILSON	1973	680'	78'	45'	33,800	American Steamship Company
PAUL THAYER	1973	630'	68'	36' 11"	19,650	Kinsman Marine Transit Company
PRESQUE ISLE (2)	1973	1000'	105'	46'6"	57,500	Litton Great Lakes Corporation
ROGER M. KYES	1973	680'	78'	42'	28,200	American Steamship Company
WILLIAM R. ROESCH	1973	630'	68'	36' 11"	19,650	Kinsman Marine Transit Company
H. LEE WHITE (2)	1974	704'	78'	45'	35,200	American Steamship Company
WOLVERINE (2)	1974	630'	68'	36' 11"	19,650	Columbia Transportation
SAM LAUD	1975	634' 10"	68'	40'	23,800	American Steamship Company
JAMES R. BARKER	1976	1004'	105'	50'	63,300	Interlake Steamship Company
JOSEPH L. BLOCK	1976	728'	78'	45'	37,200	Inland Steel Company
ST. CLAIR (2)	1976	770'	92'	52'	44,000	American Steamship Company
BELLE RIVER	1977	1000'	105'	56'	78,850	American Steamship Company
MESABI MINER	1977	1004'	105'	56'	63,300	Interlake Steamship Company
BUFFALO (3)	1978	634' 10"	68'	40'	23,800	American Steamship Company
GEORGE A. STINSON	1978	1004'	105'	50'	59,700	National Steel Corporation
LEWIS WILSON FOY	1978	1000'	105'	56'	78,850	Bethlehem Steel Corporation
EDWIN H. GOTT	1979	1004'	105'	56'	74,100	United States Steel Corporation
FRED R. WHITE JR.	1979	636'	68'	40'	23,800	Columbia Transportation
INDIANA HARBOR	1979	1000'	105'	56'	78,850	American Steamship Company
AMERICAN MARINER	1980	730'	78'	45'	37,200	American Steamship Company
BURNS HARBOR	1980	1000'	105'	56'	78,850	Bethlehem Steel Corporation
EDGAR B. SPEER	1980	1004'	105'	56'	73,700	United States Steel Corporation
AMERICAN REPUBLIC	1981	634' 10"	68'	40'	24,800	American Steamship Company
COLUMBIA STAR	1981	1000'	105'	56'	78,850	Columbia Transportation
WILLIAM J. DE LANCEY	1981	1013' 6"	105'	56'	68,000	Interlake Steamship Company

Total Single Trip Capacity: 1,326,500 Gross Tons

This chart lists all of the ships constructed between 1972 and 1981 for the US flagged fleet to operate in the bulk trades on the Great Lakes. A total of 27 ships were built during this time period which entered service for 9 separate shipping companies. Of these fleets, the American Steamship Company built 10 ships during that time period, far ahead of the its nearest rivals in ship construction which were the Bethlehem Steel Corporation, Columbia Transportation, Interlake Steamship, and the United States Steel Corporation all of which took the delivery of 3 vessels each. It is also clear from this listing that the time period in question did not only signify the construction of the thousand-foot class but also a general modernization of the US flagged fleet as a whole.

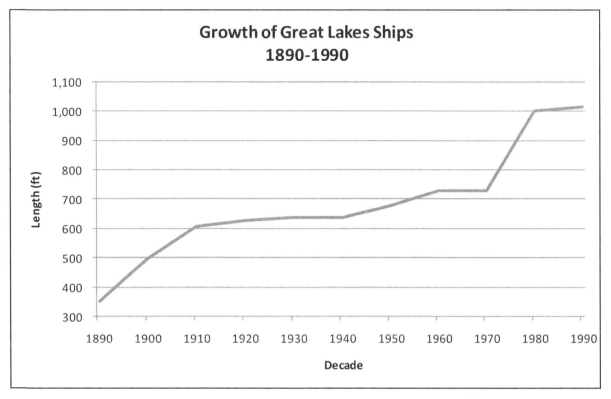

Growth of Great Lakes Ships 1890-1990

The above chart tracks the growth of Great Lakes bulk freighters over a 100 year period beginning in 1890. The figures used reflect the longest ship in service on the Great Lakes at the beginning of each decade. The time period of 1890 through 1910 represent a twenty year period in which the length of the largest ships on the lakes grew from 350-feet to just over 600-feet. After this, came a period in which ship size leveled off somewhat, although continuing to grow at a steady rate through the 1960s. During the following decade, the building of the thousand-foot vessels created a major increase in ship size as can be seen on the right hand side of the graph.

US FLAGGED VESSELS LENGTHENED DURING THE 1970s

SHIP	BUILT	ORIG. LENGTH	LENGTHENED	NEW LENGTH	YEAR	Owner
CHARLES M. BEEGHLY	1959	710'	96'	806'	1972	Interlake Steamship Company
JOHN SHERWIN (2)	1958	710'	96'	806'	1973	Interlake Steamship Company
CASON J. CALLAWAY	1952	647'	120'	767'	1974	United States Steel Corporation
PHILIP R. CLARKE	1952	647'	120'	767'	1974	United States Steel Corporation
ARMCO	1953	647'	120'	767'	1974	Columbia Transportation
ARTHUR M. ANDERSON	1952	647'	120'	767'	1975	United States Steel Corporation
RESERVE	1953	647'	120'	767'	1975	Columbia Transportation
ARTHUR B. HOMER	1960	730'	96'	826'	1975	Bethlehem Steel Corporation
JOHN G. MUNSON (2)	1952	666' 3"	102'	768' 3"	1976	United States Steel Corporation
EDWARD B. GREENE	1952	647'	120'	767'	1976	Cleveland Cliffs Steamship Company
WALTER A. STERLING	1961*	730'	96'	826'	1976	Cleveland Cliffs Steamship Company
WILLIAM CLAY FORD (1)	1953	647'	120'	767'	1979	Ford Motor Company

*=Rebuilt from a salt water tanker originally built in 1942.

During the 1970s there were 12 existing steamers which were lengthened as a result of the opening of the new Poe Lock at Sault Ste. Marie, Michigan. Following these reconstructions, none of these ships were able to transit the Welland Canal, thereby restricting them from trading any further east than Lake Erie. All of these lengthening rebuilds took place at Fraser Shipyards in Superior, Wisconsin with the exception of the reconstruction of the WALTER A. STERLING which was completed at Lorain, Ohio by the American Ship Building Company. Of these ships, only the JOHN SHERWIN (2), ARTHUR B. HOMER, and the WILLIAM CLAY FORD (1) were not later converted into self-unloaders. Consequently, the HOMER and the FORD (1) were sold for scrap in the mid-1980s, while the JOHN SHERWIN (2) has remained idle since 1981.

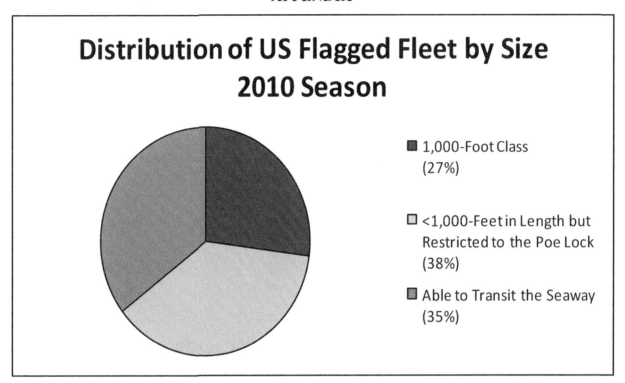

The size breakdown of the vessels in the US flagged fleet engaged in the movement of bulk materials is represented above, while the distribution of the fleet's single trip capacity is represented below. These calculations do not take into consideration any of the cement carriers and smaller barges in operation on the Great Lakes. It does however contain barge units such as the JOSEPH H. THOMPSON due to the fact that they regularly operate in the same trade patterns in which powered freighters are engaged. Illustrated here is the reliance of the US fleet upon the Poe Lock at Sault Ste. Marie, Michigan through which 65-percent of the ships in operation are required to use. As can be ascertained from the chart below, the ships of the 1,000-foot class represent nearly half of all the available capacity of the US flagged fleet. Additionally, these representations convey the importance of building a second lock at Sault Ste. Marie, Michigan with dimensions similar to that of the Poe Lock as 80% percent of the US fleet's capacity is restricted to that lock.

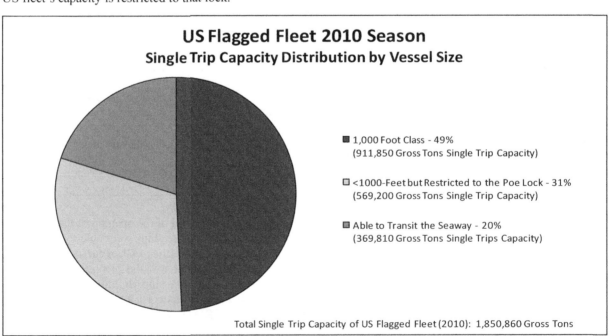

VESSEL INDEX

VESSEL INDEX

Made in the USA
Monee, IL
14 December 2023

49227873R00059